Advanced Sailing

The Design, Rigging, Handling,
Trailering, Equipping and
Maintenance of Modern Sailboats

Advanced Sailing

The Design, Rigging, Handling,
Trailering, Equipping and
Maintenance of Modern Sailboats

by Tony Gibbs

By the same author:
Practical Sailing
Pilot's Work Book/Pilot's Log Book
Powerboating
Sailing: A First Book
Backpacking

ST. MARTIN'S PRESS, NEW YORK

St. Martin's Press
175 Fifth Avenue
New York, N.Y. 10010

In Memory of Bill Birmingham, who got me into all this.

Acknowledgments
The author would like to express his
thanks to all the people who made this
book possible, most notably the crews
who have put up with me over the past
decade or so. Also to John Breault of
Hirondelle West, whose generosity made
possible the spinnaker jibing sequence;
to Don Posey of Topside Maintenance at
Marina Del Rey; and to the Nicro/Fico
Company of San Leandro, CA. Where
identifiable boats have appeared in the
illustrations, I've named the class to
which they belong, for possible
convenience to readers, but I've made
no effort to restrict the illustrations
to boats currently in production.

CONTENTS

INTRODUCTION

There are literally dozens of books, many of them excellent, that can teach a beginner how to sail. And there are even more to instruct the sailing racer in the logistics, strategy and tactics of racing. This book, however, is intended for the person who already knows sailing basics and who wants to learn more about the whys and hows of skillful sailing, without getting into competition.

While there's a great deal to be said for racing, either round-the-buoys or offshore, it's my feeling that many sailors get into racing too soon, before they've really absorbed the intricacies of sailing itself. Once on the race course, the skipper tends to judge all technique and theory according to one set of standards, and a partial one at that.

Advanced Sailing picks up in complexity more or less where my previous book, *Basic Sailing*, left off; that is, it assumes a primary knowledge of the parts of a standard sailboat and how they work. Obviously, any other beginners' sailing text will furnish an equivalent foundation. From this base, *Advanced Sailing* attempts to explore some of the current, accepted theories in sail and boat design, and show how they can be used to make your boat— whatever her hull form or rig—attain her best performance.

We will look at boat handling as an art, sailboats planing and under power, trailering, advanced seamanship, exotic equipment and rigs—all the areas of information, in short, that a man or woman should be familiar with in order to qualify as an able sailor under today's conditions.

One final word: Very little of what's in this book amounts to much until it's put into practice. Take your knowledge to sea with you, and if what you learn here makes you a more accomplished sailor, both of us will be happy.

Sunfish and Sailfish

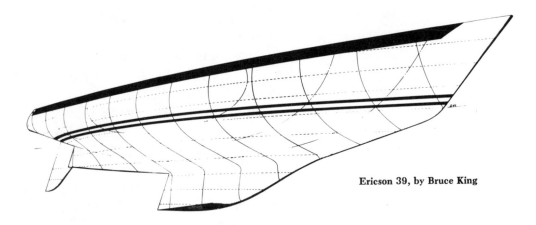

Ericson 39, by Bruce King

Part I. Modern Sailboats and Their Design

1. The Theory of Sailboat Design

It's ironic that sailing craft seem at last to be approaching a whole new plateau of development, now that they have lost all trace of material usefulness. Despite a few pitiful stragglers, the sailing vessel is no longer a part of the working economy; to reach its true potential, the sailboat had to become a toy. In part the new superboats proclaimed in the yachting press are just advertising enthusiasm, but there is a very real level of excellence, a different order of achievement here, too.

Every once in a while a designer, praised for some apparent breakthrough, will remark sheepishly that it's all been done before: fin and skeg, chine or no chine, bendy rig—someone's already thought of it, usually someone named Herreshoff. But what we are seeing today is often the realization of those designers' dreams made possible by construction materials that really are breakthroughs.

Admiral Beaufort, for instance, when defining a Force 12 storm, was able to put it in a nutshell: *that wind which no canvas can withstand*. We now have Dacron sails that will survive any wind, and this fact, curiously enough, sometimes removes an existing safety factor: instead of blowing out a sail, the modern skipper loses his rig.

Or take the case of the famous schooner *Enchantress*, described in some detail in Howard Chapelle's *American Sailing Ships*. A racing schooner of the 1880s, *Enchantress* seldom seemed able to sail up to her potential, largely because she was so very difficult to tune—and no wonder, considering the building materials available at the time. Today's sailor has so much mechanical assistance and space-age material at his disposal that he has to be warned against cranking the rig up so tight that he drives the mast down through the hull.

Despite all man's efforts, the sea that Herreshoff—or Drake—sailed on responds to the same physical laws as it always has, and the wind, though tainted with exhaust, still blows in its ordained patterns. So sailboats may function more efficiently, but the forces which govern them remain much the same. We can apply some of those forces more effectively than our fathers and grandfathers could, but those people, if they were scientists, would understand what we're trying to do.

A boat, unlike nearly every other form of transport, functions in two mediums at once. Sometimes more important, it operates at the boundary where two fluids, one 800 times as dense as the other, meet and interact. This is the most important fact to grasp in trying to understand what sailing is all about: part of the boat is in the air and part of it's under the water.

Air and water each play complementary parts in boat design. The wind, which makes the boat able to move, also attempts to drive the craft in often undesired directions; at the

Laser—a modern planing boat (Ellie Martin photo).

same time, the water which has to be forced aside to permit forward progress can also be utilized to counteract slippage of the hull to leeward. The boat designer's job, no matter what kind of boat he's creating, is to amplify the desirable attributes of each medium and minimize the undesirable ones.

There are really three pure types of boats possible: submarines, which function completely beneath the surface; displacement hulls, which operate naturally in the water and the air at once; and true planing boats, like hydroplanes, which are only marginally in contact with the water. We can forget the first category, and to understand planing as it applies to sailboats, we must radically modify some ideas about the third.

Begin with *displacement*, that much-used term. Anything that floats in water displaces an amount of water equal to its own weight.

By contraction, we have come to refer to a boat's displacement as being synonymous with weight—which it is, with a couple of footnotes we'll get into later.

Most people can get the idea of displacement easily enough by picturing a brim-full bathtub. Into this tub you gently lower a large block of wood, and over the edge flows a considerable quantity of water. If you were able to collect the overflowed water you would find that it weighed exactly as much as the block.

Afloat and at rest, all boats are displacement boats. Once they begin to move, however, matters may change. The pure displacement hull—which meant, until relatively recently, all sailboats—continues to displace its own weight of water as it proceeds. At the same time, it displaces water from its path, but the primary thing to bear in mind is that the boat itself is supported at all times by the static force of its own buoyancy.

A planing hull, on the other hand, is at first supported by buoyancy alone—is, in fact, a displacement hull while it gains speed. As the boat moves faster, it begins to emerge from the water, for reasons we'll go into, until the boat is at planing speed, supported partially by displacement and partially by the dynamic forces of its own forward motion. It's an absurd oversimplification, but a planing boat is a planing boat only when it's planing.

Planing, especially in sailing craft, is not an absolute state. A vessel which emerges completely from the water isn't a boat, in the normal sense of the word. Even the fastest planing hull is partly a displacement boat as well. This much said, it is still true that the hull characteristics required for a planing or semiplaning hull are quite different from those acceptable in a boat which is never expected to plane.

Let's examine first what makes a good displacement hull. In designing a boat, a naval architect must balance off a number of conflicting demands. Relative speed has become more and more important (though to a nonsailor, the difference between four and five knots seems pretty fine). Seaworthiness is always desirable, even in flat-water boats, but too much attention given to creating an indestructible hull may result simply in an everlasting tub. There is also the considerably different quality of seakindliness—a vessel's ability to cushion her human crew from the shocks of the sea. Accommodation has become more and more elaborate, and on smaller and smaller hulls. And finally there is still the matter of appearance, perhaps the hardest thing to pin down because the once-accepted standards of looks in a boat have changed so much and so fast.

Boat design in its performance aspect consists in emphasizing the speed-producing qualities, while minimizing the ones which contribute to slowness. This is perhaps not so simpleminded a definition as it may appear.

Generally speaking, the sails constitute a boat's main speed-producing elements: For confirmation, look to iceboats, which can achieve incredible speeds, several times the velocity of the wind. And while it does make positive contributions (such as carrying the crew), the hull is the principal source of slowness, the speed limiter.

Most sailboats—even planing ones—are very slow indeed. Their speed potential is not high, and even that low potential is seldom reached. The slowness factors holding a hull back are five in number, but two of them stand well above the rest. Collectively, the factors contributing to slowness go by the name of *resistance*.

And for most sailboats, most of the time, the main resistance factor is simply friction, hull against water. A number of authorities have calculated that the average boat spends the large majority of its sailing time operating at half to three-quarters of its potential top speed—at speed-length ratios of 0.6 to 1.0. Since the speed-length ratio is one of the basics of any discussion of hull design, it may be as well to trot it out here, for those who have not previously encountered it, or who have forgotten how it is figured.

Briefly, the speed-length ratio is simply an expression in numbers of the relationship between a boat's speed at the moment of discussion and her waterline length. Abbreviated $S/\sqrt{L}$ (sometimes $V/\sqrt{L}$), it is figured by dividing the boat's speed (in knots) by the square root of her waterline length (in feet): Thus a boat with a 16-foot waterline (the square root of which is of course 4), sailing at two knots, has a speed-length ratio of 0.5. If she accelerates to four knots, her $S/\sqrt{L}$ becomes 1.0, and at five knots it is 1.25.

At low boat speeds—the most usual speeds, remember—surface friction accounts for most of the hull resistance. In his authoritative book, *Sailing Theory and Practice*,* C. A. Marchaj described tests carried out in the controlled conditions of a towing tank on the full size hull of an International Canoe. At a speed of two knots, friction accounted for over 90 per cent of the total resistance on the 17-foot hull; not until the boat was moving at about 5-1/2 knots did the other causes of hull resistance (discussed later) equal friction.

The International Canoe is, to be sure, something of a special case, one of the lightest of the lightweight hulls. Another authority, Douglas Phillips-Birt, figures that in a very light-displacement racer-cruiser, friction accounts for 75 per cent of the resistance at $0.8 \, S/\sqrt{L}$, 70 per cent at 0.9, 65 per cent at 1.0, 51 per cent at 1.1 and 37 per cent at 1.2. For a more orthodox, heavy-displacement hull, Mr. Phillips-Birt gives skin friction

resistance as 75 per cent of the total with a $S/\sqrt{L}$ of 0.4, down to about 50 per cent at 0.9.

Bear in mind that these percentages represent parts of the total resistance—which itself continues to climb as the boat gains speed. Skin friction thus varies according to speed, and also according to area of wetted surface, smoothness of surface and length of surface.

At this point in design history, wetted surface area is the most important of the four factors contributing to skin friction, and it is wetted surface which has been under the most continuous design attack in recent years. There is, as we shall see in the next chapter, a design conflict between the achievement of minimum wetted surface and the most efficient underwater shape for balance and stability. For the moment, it's enough to consider each new sailboat hull in terms of how the designer has come to grips with the problem of reducing wetted surface as much as possible (and it *is* possible to overdo, in terms of cutting away so much underbody that the boat fails in some other design area).

We must accept the climb of skin friction with increased speed, at least insofar as it is a fact of physics, just as we have to swallow the increase of friction with length (although a longer hull's skin friction is not proportionally greater than a short one's).

The new point of attack for designers attempting to reduce the effect of skin friction—egged on, of course, by racers—is in the area of hull smoothness. For many years it has been an article of sailing faith that a boat's bottom was as functionally smooth as it could get when human fingertips could feel no roughness. People sanded and sanded their hulls to incredible smoothness, scrubbed them before races or hauled them altogether between contests. It was perfectly obvious that a smoother hull below the waterline meant a faster boat. What could be more logical?

HEAVY DISPLACEMENT YACHT

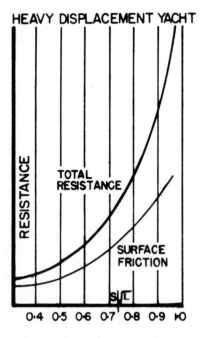

Skin friction as a component of total resistance.

*Sailing Theory and Practice (New York: Dodd, Mead Co., 1964).

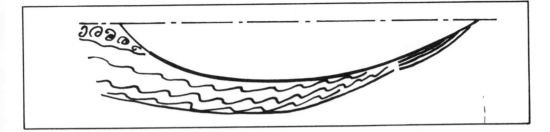

Laminar flow is possible over the forward part of the hull, but turbulence increases the further aft you go.

Some skippers went beyond ordinary smoothness, experimenting with textures —such as lampblack, grease or wax—that suggested additional smoothness over and beyond the normal definition. A sailor might get a psychological boost from applying a "secret" go-fast goo, but the effect on the boat's bottom seemed at best not proven either way. For all intents and purposes, a bottom finish equivalent to that on highly polished furniture seemed as good as any (and not so easy to achieve or maintain, either).

There were still no dramatic breakthroughs, in part because of the nature of friction along hulls. When a boat moves through the water, it does not simply shear the liquid as a razor blade shears paper. Rather, a boat remains enveloped as it moves in a thin layer of water which is carried along with the hull. In this very thin boundary layer, water speeds vary. At the hull surface, the water molecules are moving forward just about at boat speed, and as the distance from the hull increases, the water speed decreases.

It's obviously very hard to pinpoint the effective thickness of a boat's boundary layer. The British designer-author Maurice Griffiths has estimated that the actual laminar film, the layer of water moving at the same speed as the boat, is a few thousandths of an inch in thickness, while the boundary layer, which widens moving from bow to stern, may be as much as five inches thick at maximum. As the boat presses forward, the disturbance of its passage is transmitted from the laminar film outward, producing a turbulence in the boundary layer. Much of the skin friction effect on the boat derives from this turbulence.

When a boat with a very smooth and well-shaped hull moves through the water at normal displacement-sailing speeds, the boundary layer over most of the hull is characterized by this normal turbulence. But it is possible to eliminate, at least here and there, turbulence in the boundary layer, replacing it with what is called *laminar flow*, a condition in which the boundary layer is divided into unmixing, parallel sublayers, each one from hull outward moving at a slightly lower speed. There is frictional resistance remaining, but it derives from shearing between the layers, and it produces much less drag—only a sixth as much, says Griffiths—than ordinary turbulent flow.

Under the most favorable conditions today, laminar flow can be achieved on the forward part of a good hull, and over most of a well-designed and maintained fin keel or centerboard. Obviously, if it were possible to extend laminar control over the rest of the wetted surface, a real breakthrough in speed would take place—the skin friction resistance of a normal displacement yacht might be reduced from a couple of hundred pounds to less than fifty. No wonder architects and skippers have been circling hungrily around the problem, attacking it from a number of points at once.

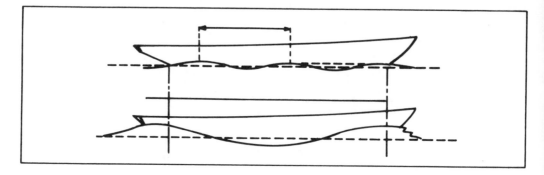

As a boat's speed increases, so does the length between the crests of its wave system. Lower drawing is at hull speed.

There is no solution yet, and the architects seem to have gone about as far as they can in producing low-friction shapes. Right now, the best chances seem to lie in one (or perhaps both) of two directions. First is simply the chemical school, the people who still believe that some new composition applied to the hull will produce near-total hydrodynamic smoothness. This kind of alchemy may, with our present-day knowledge, prove out; the most promising developments appear to be in the continual release while under way of a liquid coating from the bow. This system has already received the accolade of being banned by the rule makers, just as multihulls and fully battened sails were in their time. So maybe it does work.

The other course is more ambitious: Proceeding from the theory that certain fish (notably dolphins) have control over their own boundary layers, people have begun reexamining the nature of marine animals' skins; can flexibility be the answer, cushioning the boat's passage through the water and thus preventing breaking of the laminar flow? Maybe.

For now, however, laminar flow is very much in the nature of a distant grail, except as it operates on partial areas of the hull, and—in that other fluid—across a boat's sails.

But all the efforts at reducing skin friction, whether by smoothing the skin or eliminating roughness, merely transfer the resistance problem to another arena. For if skin friction is the major drag at low speeds, wave-making is the important factor as the boat's speed increases.

Go back to the speed-length ratio for a moment. You may have read somewhere that a displacement hull's maximum potential speed—her *hull speed*—is in the area of 1.4 times the $\sqrt{LWL}$, or when the boat's speed-length ratio is 1.4. You may also have heard that, for a pure displacement hull, additional power does little or no good, once this magic speed is achieved. The boat simply squats, seemingly falling into a hole in the water.

This is more or less the case. What happens is that any hull moving through water creates two wave patterns. One consists of what we usually think of as the wake—the waves radiating at an angle from bow and stern. These waves are of primary concern to other boats. What counts is the series of transverse waves, moving in the same direction as the boat and at right angles to its centerline.

A slow-moving boat creates one group of waves at the bow and another group at the quarter. These are separate wave systems, moving at the same speed as the boat. As the boat's speed increases, so does the speed of the waves—but the distance between crests gets longer too. At a speed-length ratio of about 1.25 or so, the boat's waterline length begins to coincide with the wavelength, so that the boat is riding in a trough of its own creation. The only way to escape is for the boat suddenly to pull itself up and over its own bow wave—a situation called *surfing*, which can happen with lightweight displacement hulls for brief periods, and under fairly specialized conditions.

Not only does a lightweight boat respond more readily to additional surges of power, but it also, by reason of its hull form, creates a shallower wave system than does a heavy-displacement boat. The waves are as long, for boats of the same LWL at the same speed, but the light-displacement boat's wave system is not so hard to climb over.

And finally, of course, one arrives at the planing boats, which are able, because of lightness and hull shape, to climb over their bow waves with regularity, and assume a planing attitude. It's important to remember that the planing mode doesn't decrease drag on the hull. Rather, it lessens the increase of resistance, as the chart shows.

The hull shapes of planing and displacement hulls are obviously quite different, as we shall see in the next chapter. But even when two hulls may look the same, their construction can be so different that the boats in question have little in common.

2. Modern Sailing Hulls

As we saw in the first chapter, one purpose of hull design is to minimize resistance. Obviously, the less hull there is in the water, the less resistance there will be—but right here we come into conflict with the two reasons for there to be a formal hull at all: load carrying, and stability of the entire boat. Providing a moving container for goods, crew and gear was, of course, the reason boats came into being in the first place. As commercial sail yielded almost completely to pleasure boating, it was possible and even reasonable to scrap nearly all the load-carrying requirement in the search for speed. Still, most sailors retained a desire to cart along with them a number of necessities and a few extras—and the amount involved can easily be seen at haul-out time, when even a small cruising sloop can disgorge an entire station-wagon load of material.

The hull also provides a platform on which to erect the rig: A certain amount of strength, length and beam are necessary simply to stay a tall mast properly, and in most boats, the shape of the hull is one of the elements contributing to the boat's total stability—its ability to keep from capsizing from the force of the wind on the sails.

For convenience' sake, let's begin by dividing all sailboat hulls into two main categories (even though such a division means oversimplifying a bit). We can call these *ballasted* and *nonballasted* hulls, though nowadays one could make a reasonable argument for naming the same categories *displacement* and *planing*. To be sure, there are a number of boats falling more or less between our two poles, but it will help to look at the nearly pure forms first, then go on to the compromises.

Bear in mind as we examine hull forms that

they don't exist in isolation. Everything on a sailboat interacts with everything else, and while it may be necessary to consider one part at a time, the hull or the rig or the steering are only parts of a coherent whole.

In the opinion of many authorities, some of them naval architects, the overall design of displacement hulls has gone about as far as it can, given the materials and construction methods of the present and the foreseeable future. There may—almost certainly will —continue to be refinements, but the theme itself is fixed.

Displacement hulls today are more and more restricted to larger craft, especially to boats with cruising accommodations. There remain obvious exceptions, led by the 12-Meter sloops, but while the Establishment of yachting concentrates on the refinement of detail in these vessels, the real development of speed under sail is in the area of nonballasted hulls. The visible activity in displacement hull design seems to consist mostly in taking advantage of the inevitable split between all-out distance racers on the one hand and the new, not-quite-motorsailer cruising yachts on the other.

Today's displacement hulls reflect this split, though the boats themselves still form a spectrum, with no clear separation point where cruising design ends and pure racing begins. Yacht design, as a separate intellectual exercise, is little more than a century old. Although pleasure sailboats date back at least three hundred years and probably more, until the 1850s they were simply small commercial craft, slightly altered to function in a slightly different fashion.

There's no space here to go into the history of yacht design, fascinating as it is.* Suffice it to say that by the turn of the twentieth century, yacht designers had experimented

*Interested readers may want to consult *Sailing Yacht Design*, by Douglas Phillips-Birt (Camden, Maine, International Marine Publishing Co., 1966).

with most of the available forms. More important, the scientific principles behind resistance and stability had not only been discovered but, to a large extent, agreed upon. From this point, further development hinged on three factors: 1. The type of design compromise forced by the owners' requirements; 2. The steady development of new marine materials; and 3. The requirements of the various racing handicapping rules.

Yacht handicapping is a lot more complicated than loading a fast horse with lead weights. Since boats (unlike horses) can be designed to take advantage of any handicapping rule, the rule itself becomes not only more complex, but also anticipatory: that is, the creators of the rule, knowing it will be applied to boats not yet designed, attempt to force future designs into a direction which the rule-makers themselves find congenial. (Rule-makers call this "encouraging wholesome boats," but since most of them are actively engaged in the commercial production of these boats, another term, such as stacking the deck, might seem more applicable.)

I've gone onto this small sidetrack to suggest that when certain aspects of design seem irrational, they often are—reflecting not reality, but the artificial parameters of a handicap system.

To examine the functions of a sailing hull, it may help to take three different views —profile, waterline, and midship section—to see what each can tell us. The profile, both above and below the waterline, is the most dramatic, and it shows most clearly the design changes over the past half-century.

As the series of profiles shows, the great trend above the waterline has been shortening the boat's overhangs, while the underwater shape of the displacement hull has simply diminished until it is now, in some designs, at an irreducible minimum. Overhangs in a hull have both advantages and drawbacks; properly executed, an overhanging prow with a relatively sharp entry can part the seas smoothly and help to reduce pounding. The old-fashioned spoon bows, with their accompanying low freeboard, made for a wet boat that was virtually uninhabitable forward. But the primary function of a bow or stern overhung beyond the waterline was simply to provide extra length when the boat was heeled, and hence extra speed potential not

theme, although not with any resounding commercial success. There's nothing essentially wrong with this hull shape for a modern cruiser—it's not quite as fast as it might be, but it's a good load carrier. Draft, for some areas, may be a bit much (although skippers spend far more time worrying about draft, in my opinion, than they need to).

A fairly similar, albeit shallower, hull is

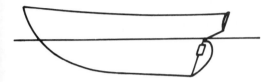

Earliest yachts, like this one, were derived from commercial sail craft.

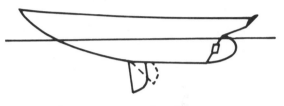

More reduction in wetted surface was achieved by lessening depth of the keel.

taxed under a rating system. As the system has closed most of the loopholes, ends have become correspondingly shorter.

Underwater, it was at first thought that a boat's entire lateral plane was of equal effect in resisting leeway, and the first designer to cut away the bow substantially endured a storm of ridicule—until his boat, deprived not

easy to work out, by merely removing some more underbody along the keel, replacing the missing lateral surface by a centerboard. As you may have known—or may be beginning to suspect—this reduction in draft will cause some changes in the boat's shape elsewhere, as we shall see.

The keel-centerboard boat has achieved much popularity, especially since fiberglass construction made centerboard trunks so

The first step in reducing underbody was to cut away the forefoot, as here.

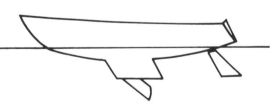

The keel-centerboard hull avoids having a trunk intrude into the living spaces.

of effective lateral area, but of draggy wetted surface, walked away from other craft. The cutaway bow lost the boat a little buoyancy forward, but not a great deal of usable interior space. Deck length and beam were just as great.

This type of hull is still popular today. Even an occasional new boat is designed to this

much more resistant to leaking. In this type of design, one has a board of reasonable size which is housed beneath the accommodation even when fully raised. More important, there is the option of changing the boat's balance by raising and lowering the board—really moving the pivoting centerboard forward and aft. There are still problems with keel-centerboard boats, as there are with everything. Banged hard enough, the board may bend or split the trunk; the pennant may snap or the centerboard winch foul; mud or stones may jam the board halfway up or down; a centerboard, in boats of cruising size, may run a thousand dollars or more than a keel hull of equivalent displacement.

The next step in profile design takes us to the now-familiar fin-keel/spade-rudder combination, coupled with minimal wetted surface. The fin, rather than fairing gently into the main body of the hull, is a stark out-

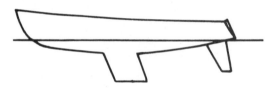

Familiar to everyone by now, this fin keel/spade rudder conformation is probably the most common today in keel boats.

growth—often bolted directly onto a hull of otherwise semicircular profile. The fin keel was invented in the last century—and utilized in the America's Cup, too—but the considerable strains it imposed on the hull plus the lack of seakindliness of the arrangement stopped its development. Now we can build such a boat easily, and enough hard-case racers don't care about seakindliness so that there's a market for the boat.

One item about fin keels worth mentioning. Such a design virtually requires a detached (although not necessarily spade-shaped) rudder, located well aft to provide more leverage on the hull. A rudder so placed, without a protective skeg and subjected to severe stresses, is prone to failure of

one sort or another. In addition, it tends to emerge as the boat heels, causing runaways and broaches, especially in brisk conditions when reaching or running under too much sail.

With the advent of a mass market for trailerable cruisers, there has arrived a variant on the fin-keel boat in which the keel is pivoted at its forward end. It retracts, usually into a stub keel that may extend partly into the

For trailerable cruisers, the retractable keel is popular. It locks up or down.

accommodation. More important, the keel is not like a centerboard, because it's locked either all the way up or all the way down, *and* it is significantly weighted. These swing-keel boats are extremely light and sail like well-designed daysailers, but they are, of course, limited in beam (and thus in the other dimensions) by the laws regarding highway trailer widths.

One other type of keel hull may be worth mentioning, although it's not too different in

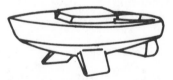

The twin keel boat will sit level on the bottom, but it drags a great deal of underbody along with it.

shape from a standard fin keel boat, and that's the twin keeler. The two keels, angled at about 30° to each other, allow the boat to ride on an even keel (perhaps it should be *keels*) when sitting on the bottom. Although the twin-keel adherents can be counted on to claim that their boats are superior performers afloat as well as aground, this does not seem to be the case—nor is it surprising. In wetted surface alone the twin-keel hull lugs around considerably more area than her single-keel cousin, not to mention what must be a singular amount of turbulence between the two keels and the follow-on protective skeg and rudder. Where sitting on the bottom in a genteel fashion is of major importance, the twin-keel boat has achieved some popularity, but in most areas her generally conceded lack of speed and relatively poor ability to windward are crushing penalties.

Looking at boats from the side is informative. Almost as useful is cutting them in two crosswise and examining the midships cross section, which is the key section in the design.

Let's begin well back in time, with a cross section that might correspond to the first of our profiles or indeed to an even older boat. This sort of midship section is seldom seen today, and even less frequently designed. Although its wetted surface is not especially great as a section, a shape like this requires that the remainder of the boat's underbody be full as well, barring the development of any considerable amount of cutting away of the hull.

In addition, it has been proven that an underbody of this general shape is very inefficient going to windward, a point which will become clearer when we get to the newer boats that are good close-hauled. From this early shape developed the familiar wineglass cross section, in which the keel is faired into the hull, while the fin aspect becomes more pronounced. In the same size boat, the effective ballast is considerably lower than with the nearly keelless form, although the hull itself is visibly trending away from load-carrying, in favor of pure sailing efficiency.

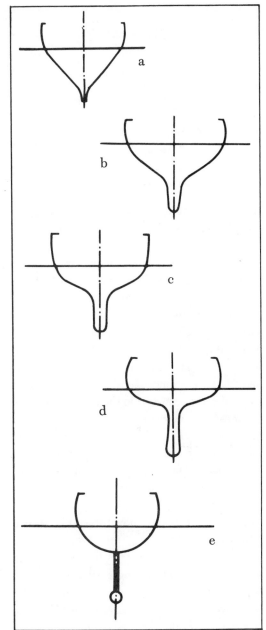

From top to bottom, the cross-sections illustrate reduction in wetted surface and progress toward the complete fin: (a) has only a slight keel shape, while in (b) the turn of the bilge is more pronounced: (c) is a true wineglass, and (d) could be called a champagne glass shape: (e) is a semicircular hull section with a fin—weighted, in this case.

13

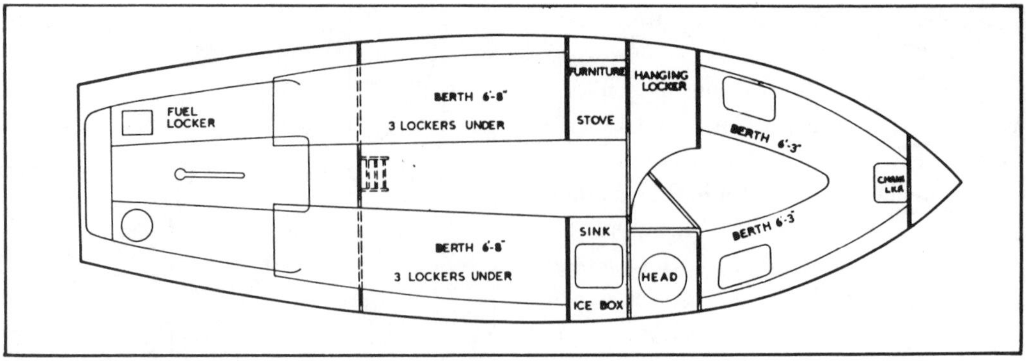
FUEL
LOCKER
BERTH 6'-8"
3 LOCKERS UNDER
BERTH 6'-8"
3 LOCKERS UNDER
FURNITURE
STOVE
HANGING
LOCKER
SINK
ICE BOX
HEAD
BERTH 6'-3"
BERTH 6'-3"

Outline of a Westerly Nomad cruiser shows once-popular cod's head/mackerel stern.

The wineglass also appears in a much more pronounced form, which Richard Henderson* calls *champagne glass*: the hull is relatively beamier, with a pronounced turn to the bilges—almost a chine, in some cases—while the keel itself is now very obviously a fin. Looked at simply in cross section, a boat of this type would seem to have far more wetted surface, just from the extra area of the in-and-down curve of hull and fin. This would be true *if* the fin ran the length of the boat—but of course it doesn't. This section corresponds to the fin-keel/spade-rudder conformation, and what wetted surface is added in the midship section is more than compensated for by removal of wetted surface elsewhere.

Last stop on this route is the semicircular hull with fin, a logical progression because the semicircular cross section (by itself) has the least wetted surface of any shape. The keel may concentrate the ballast in a torpedo-shaped bulb, as in the Star or the Half-ton Scampi class, but generally speaking, bulbs have not been as successful as placing the ballast in the lowest part of the keel proper.

These are all round or rounded hulls. A successful displacement hull need not be rounded—look at the Star—and there are certain advantages to hard-chine hulls. First, this shape allows for relatively inexpensive construction in sheet plywood, something which seemed more attractive a few years ago than it does now. More important, a displacement boat with a nearly flat bottom and fin keel can have both limited wetted surface and a high degree of initial stability, conferred by the hull shape. Boats of this shape tend, however, to pound rather badly and they are not considered good sea boats—uncomfortable unless fined out forward, and then apt to be wet. As daysailers they can work quite well—although here the keel militates against them, since the majority of daysailers operate close to shore, in waters that tend to be shoal.

The third view of our displacement hull is of the waterline shape. Early theorists in the field of naval architecture argued in favor of what was termed the "cod's head—mackerel tail" hull shape: heavy forward, with big shoulders and a bluff entry, fining down aft. The idea was that if a fish shaped like this could swim rapidly, a boat could go fast too. But of course a boat is—as stated earlier—a creature of two mediums.

Another school turned to the so-called symmetrical hull. In this design, the shape of the waterline is more or less the same at either end of the boat. They theory behind this shape has to do with the boat's waterline when heeled. As a hull inclines, its shape at the waterline changes, especially in boats with a

*Richard Henderson, *The Racing-Cruiser*, (Chicago: Reilly and Lee, 1970).

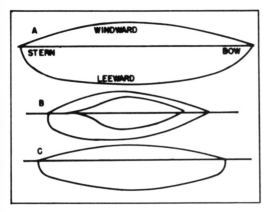

Immersed hull shape changes as the boat heels: These three waterline outlines show shape of (a) a modern hull with short ends, (b) a racer with sharp bow, full stern, (c) a symmetrical hull, with very long ends.

pronounced turn to the bilge. The drawing showing a midships section with the "in-wedge" and "out-wedge" suggests the nature of shape changes in the immersed hull.

As a symmetrical hull heels, it does change its outline, but the essential symmetry remains, in the sense that while the immersed area to leeward increases and that to windward decreases, the relative curves on either side of the centerline mirror each other at bow and stern. In theory this shape is conducive to a well-balanced, easily steered hull, and this

Paceship 23, a Hunt-designed racer-cruiser, has fine bows and load-carrying beam aft.

does seem to be the case. According to other authorities, including the American designer Ted Brewer, a symmetrical hull shape also leads to excessive pitching, because of the relatively full bow and fine stern. The bow lifts easily to oncoming waves, while the stern has insufficient area to damp out the motion.

One answer which has come to dominate hull shapes today among offshore racers is the asymmetrical hull with a fine entry and full stern. The long, lean forebody (frequently coupled with a slight flare in the bow) pushes the boat's maximum beam to a point aft of amidships, with relatively full stern sections aft. The theory here is that this shape, which carries the boat's center of buoyancy perhaps 55 per cent of the LWL from the bow, lessens pitching by reducing buoyancy forward, while adding to it aft. It is also, of course, an optimum shape for encouraging laminar flow.

The heeled waterline shape shows a large bulge to leeward and aft, which provides damping support and extra buoyancy for the crew in the cockpit—a movable weight of considerable significance in most smaller boats.

We have then a sort of composite picture of the contemporary displacement hull designed for speed: in profile, a shoal, cutaway hull with a deep fin keel and a separate rudder, probably mounted on a protecting skeg. The midship section will show a more or less semicircular curve of hull, perhaps flattened at the bottom, or with the suggestion of a

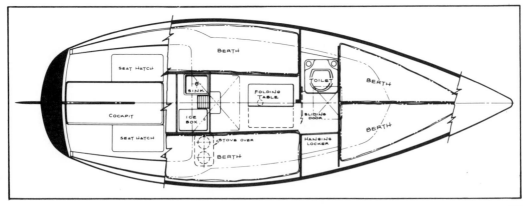

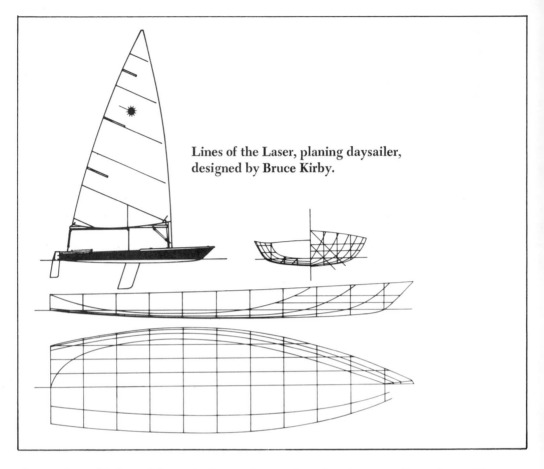

Lines of the Laser, planing daysailer, designed by Bruce Kirby.

chine, for added stability. And at the waterline, a long, slender bow and fattish, rounded stern.

The cruising hull, by contrast, has not changed so much in recent years. It still adheres more to the wine glass section, with fuller bows for more usable room forward, and a longish keel (at least in some cases) for easier steering, especially off the wind. Cruising sailboats may occasionally surf, but the experience is often under such alarming conditions that no one aboard is anxious to repeat it. Offshore racers, by comparison, are now designed and built so light that surfing can be a regular and anticipated part of their performance. It's not easy to get a ballasted boat to plane, but by using such exotica as weighted drop keels it has now become possible.

But the planing sailboat, by and large, is still a creature of flat water, still an unballasted daysailer. Without the necessity of carrying much of anything in the way of gear, without the need for a hull which will stand up to offshore battering, and with the very essential element of live ballast in relatively large amounts, today's planing sailboats are commonplace.

The most popular of all, in terms of numbers, are the various boardboats, led by the Sunfish and Sailfish. Here hull design has achieved an elegant simplicity that would be hard to beat. The boat is simply a large, wind-powered surfboard, with a flat bottom curving gently upward at the bow. The boat is easy to plane, and since it weighs less than the average one-man crew, its hard-chine hull can stand up to an extraordinary force of wind, when balanced by the hiked-out helmsman.

The drawbacks of a hull like the average boardboat—wide forward, tapering aft, with absolutely minimal freeboard—is that it can be stopped in its tracks by any kind of sea, and its flat bottom will pound in even a small chop. But as long as the crew can take it, the boat can handle its own end.

More elaborate planing hulls, such as the Laser, shown here, achieve dramatic results essentially by refining the boardboard hull, and adding a far more efficient sailing rig. The wide, flat-bottomed hull, the low freeboard, pronounced chine, light weight—all are in the same vein. Differences are the fined-out bow, the shaped quarters to reduce turbulence aft.

The ultrafast planing monohull, then, has assumed what is probably close to its own apotheosis of design in boats which resemble the racing canoe—light, narrow, flat-bottomed, dependent upon human ballast. There is one obvious avenue open, and that is to reintroduce the hull as a stability element, so that more sail can be carried.

Lines of the Iroquois, a very fast racing-cruising catamaran of 30 feet, designed by Rod Macalpine-Downie.

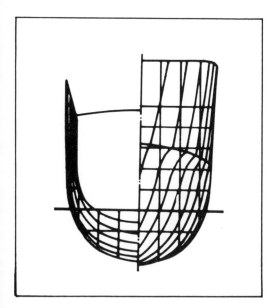

And that leads to multihulls, or in the smaller sizes, to catamarans. Narrow forward and not a great deal wider aft, the modern high-speed cat hull often has a semicircular midship section, for minimum wetted surface, a pronounced knuckle forward, to prevent the bow rooting, and somewhat flattened sections aft for crew support. With ultralight hulls and trampoline, the cat is extremely light for its length, while its great beam and its two-hull configuration give it an extremely high degree of initial stability. As a practical daysailing form, the racing catamaran is now clearly in the forefront of hull design, with only two potential competitors.

One is the proa, a development of the cat, in which one of the two hulls is reduced in size to the point where it is only a float. Sailed with this junior hull airborne, a proa has achieved more than 30 knots, to become officially the fastest boat under sail (not counting iceboats, of course).

The other challenger is the hydrofoil-supported hull, which has been well developed in power boats, but which has been held back in sailing craft by mechanical problems: the hydrofoils must be at a constant height relative to the water, and as yet a reliable adjusting system is out of sight.

Where speed under sail is only a part of the design picture, multihulls have much to offer, although their real potential is obscured as yet. For one thing, multihulls—both catamarans and trimarans—rely on ultra-lightweight construction, which is by its nature more difficult to accomplish than easy going heavy planking. So there is an exaggerated lag between what a designer puts on paper and what the builder can actually put in the water. In addition, a state of guerrilla warfare exists between mono- and multihull people (designers *and* sailors): the extreme views really exclude rational discussion—*no multihull is acceptably safe offshore* on the

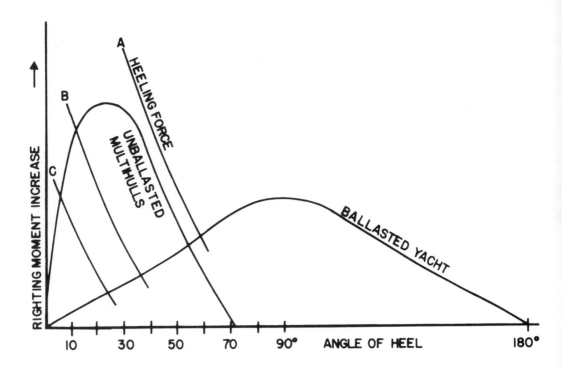

RIGHTING MOMENT INCREASE

ANGLE OF HEEL

HEELING FORCE

UNBALLASTED MULTIHULLS

BALLASTED YACHT

10   30   50   70   90°   180°

A   B   C

Relative stability of ballasted monohulls and unballasted multihulls at increasing wind strengths (A, B and C). Note steeply rising and falling multihull righting moment compared to their gradual increase of righting force to 90° in monohulls.

one hand, and *all monohulls are hopeless clunks* on the other. As there are many more monohull folk about, multihullists often retreat into paranoia, having abandoned the attempt at conversion. Sometimes their point seems well taken, as when a highly placed Olympic official, after commenting on the remarkable performance of the Tornado catamaran, added, "But of course it's not really *sailing*, you know."*

Anyway. A multihull derives all its stability from its hull form—that is, from the collective shape and arrangement of its two or three

*Conversation with the author, 1972.

hulls (plus, in smaller boats, crew weight). Once that shape stability is overcome, a multihull will capsize completely, and will attempt to remain upside down. It boils down to a contest between initial stability, in the multihull case, and ultimate stability in the case of the monohull. The graph shows the relative amounts of stability in each type of hull at varying degrees of heel.

Another multihullists' argument is that a ballasted monohull, once holed, will go down like a rock, while a multihull can be badly mauled and still stay afloat, there being no great weight aboard to pull it down. This depends, of course, on the multihull's having been built of floating material or with integral flotation, but it is certainly a point worth considering.

Nearly all trimarans are cruising boats—in the sense that they have accommodations—because the trimaran shape does not really make much sense until the boat is fairly large. The current thinking in fast trimarans calls for a long main hull, fat above the waterline and relatively thin below, with very narrow wing hulls which barely touch the water—or don't touch at all, in some cases——when the boat is at rest. With wind in the sails, only one wing hull will be in the water anyway, giving the boat the performance aspect of the proa.

To go into accommodation of cruising boats in any detail would really require another book. For a real discussion of what can—and should—be fitted into a sailing cruiser, the reader may want to consult Henderson's *The Racing-Cruiser*, referred to above, his *The Cruiser's Compendium, The Proper Yacht*, by Arthur Beiser, or some similar volume.*

3. The Sloop Rig

Why the sloop?

Why, to be more precise, has this one arrangement of spars and sails achieved such overwhelming popularity in the larger day-sailer and cruising classes? The possible alternatives number in the dozens; the *practical* alternatives comprise a half-dozen well-proved combinations. But the single-stick rig with jib and mainsail as the basic combination is the standard, except in the very smallest and largest types.

Partly the answer is that in medium-sized pleasure sailboats—say 15 to 30 feet overall -the plain vanilla sloop provides a combination of aerodynamic efficiency, flexibility of sail plan, and handling ease seldom equaled by other rigs. Part of the answer is simply availability: try buying something else. Try finding—boardboats aside—a widespread class that isn't sloops. Perhaps the best way of defining a sloop's advantages is by examining in principle what a modern sailboat must do,

then looking more closely at what the various rigs have to offer.

Most modern sailboats aim at a logical compromise in performance over the several points of sailing. Each of the basic three points—beating, reaching, running—calls for something different in hull and sailplan, and in some cases the demands are mutually exclusive: A boat wholeheartedly conceived for running is not likely to be a great success hard on the wind. So the first decision one has to make is the relative importance of each point of sailing. (Obviously this decision involves hull design as well as rig.)

The single most important requirement of a modern sailing rig is that it carry the boat efficiently to windward. This seems at first an absurdly narrow criterion. After all, sailing close-hauled accounts for only a little more than a quarter of the possible courses—or does it?

Most people still cleave to the definition of close-hauled as sailing approximately 45° to the true wind, so that allowing an extra 5° on either side, one might say that 100° out of a possible 360° in course directions called for sailing close-hauled, either in one long leg or tracking to a mark directly to windward. Peter Johnson, in *Ocean Racing and Offshore Yachts*,* says that the percentage of windward courses is actually 33, since he considers 60° on either side of the true wind as sailing more or less to windward, in terms of requirements of boat and rig design.

Indeed, one might add that with the reduced speed of sailing close-hauled, and the greater distance to cover, because of tacking, the actual *time* spent knocking the boat to windward approaches half the time spent sailing—a figure that will seem only too true to a great many cruising skippers. And as far as racers are concerned, the standard Olympic

*See Bibliography, p. 151

*Peter Johnson, *Ocean Racing & Offshore Yachts* (New York: Dodd, Mead Co., 1970).

19

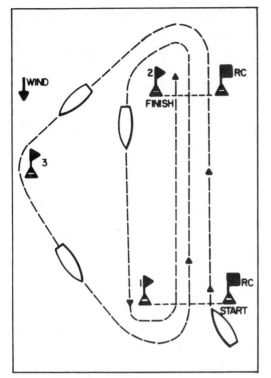

Standard Olympic-pattern closed racing course, with three windward legs, two reaches and one run, has had some influence in yacht design.

course (shown in the illustration) consists of 55 per cent windward work: Most racers feel that you win a race close-hauled—though you may lose it on another point of sailing.

So unless you sail in the Leeward Islands, it's important that your sailboat have at least reasonable windward ability. This means a hull form that resists leeway and that moves easily into headseas. It also means a sail plan that provides maximum lift, the most efficient low-speed airfoil possible. A combination of modern scientific thinking and fairly regressive rule-making has led inevitably to the high aspect ratio* sloop with a masthead or near-masthead jib. Thanks largely to the spinnaker, which has become a basic of any sail wardrobe, the sloop can be adapted to perform well off the wind, even if she is not as

easy to handle as a natural reaching rig like the ketch or schooner.

We'll talk more about sail shapes in Chapter 5, but before doing so, it may be a good idea to examine what holds the sails up, the sparring system.

Today's spars bear a superficial resemblance to the tree trunks from which they have developed. Wood masts are still sentimental favorites with many sailors, especially those of the cruising persuasion, but the decision between aluminum and wood scarcely exists for most of us, as nearly all stock boats come with metal masts as standard.

There are several good reasons. Given spars of equal cross-sectional size, aluminum is stronger, lighter, stiffer, cheaper and easier to maintain than wood. If you are in the market for a bendy spar, aluminum bends more consistently than wood, although a wood spar's bend can be changed by judicious planing.

In designing an aluminum mast, there are three basic approaches one may take. Because aluminum's strength derives partly from its wall thickness and partly from its diameter, a builder may achieve desired strength in a mast by making it in a large diameter with thin walls, in a small diameter with thick walls, or in a small diameter with thin walls and extra staying to make up for the mast's design weakness. This last route is generally unacceptable today because the overstayed mast—the kind of jumper- and strut-festooned spar that inspired the term *Marconi rig*—creates not only a sizable

*Aspect ratio is one of those shorthand phrases thrown casually about by boating writers and designers. The ratio involved is that between the luff of the mainsail in a given rig, and the mainsail foot. Thus, a sail with a luff twice the length of the foot has an aspect ratio of 2:1. Sometimes the second figure, always understood to be 1, is left out. What makes a given aspect ratio high depends on who's talking, but most people will agree that a ratio of 3:1 or more qualifies as high.

amount of extra windage but also causes considerable turbulence in the airflow.

Like most elements of boat design, the mast winds up a compromise between diameter and wall thickness; its cross-sectional shape is likely to be that of a flattened tube, with the long axis fore-and-aft, where the most strain lies. High quality spars may be

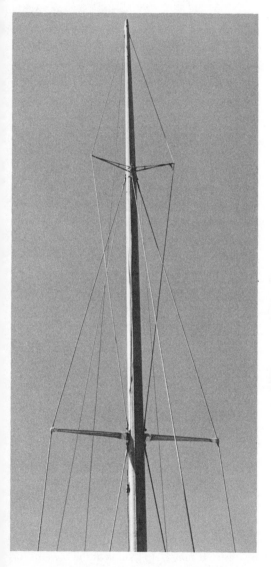

The mast of this older yacht carries enough wire aloft to make for a substantial amount of windage, not to mention some elaborate tuning problems.

tapered toward the top, both in diameter and in wall thickness. The pressure on a mast is compression, and it is greatest in the bottom section, so the length above the spreaders can be thinned out to reduce weight aloft and windage.

Even the most perfectly designed mast section is never at the optimum angle to the wind (except when the boat's riding to anchor or powering to windward)—unless, of course, the spar is made to pivot. Pivoting spars being out of bounds for most of us, we must make the best of what we have by minimizing the turbulence caused by the mast and its attachments, and by making the most efficient connection between the after edge of the mast and the mainsail luff.

Today's offshore fleet presents any number of illustrations of the lengths (and expense) one may go to in order to smooth the airflow around the mast. Halyards have been internal for some years now, but recently tangs have

Not only racers have lots of winches. These, on the cabin top of the Valiant 40 cutter, handle the mainsheet and the halyards for main, forestaysail and jib.

moved inside the spar too. The batteries of winches that racers seem unable to live without have come down off the mast to locations on deck—although this is as much to lower the weight as to reduce the windage. The ideal remains a tapered spar, with only the most essential weights aloft, and with little or nothing to obstruct the smooth run of air over its surface.

The moving air cannot follow the curve of the mast without eddying at least somewhat on the after side. This must be accepted to a degree, but what's more important to the keen windward sailor is maintaining the pressure difference between the windward and leeward sides of the sail.

As every stableboy knows, what lifts a boat to windward in the first place is the low pressure on the forward third of the sail's leeward side. Sail fabric is relatively nonporous, so the high pressure air on the windward side of the sail must stay unequalized—unless it can pass between the mast and the mainsail luff. This is why the best luff attachment is a groove in the after edge of the mast—sometimes the join between sail and spar is faired by pulling the lips of the groove back. When carried to its logical extreme, you get the wing mast, in which a sizable percentage of the airfoil is solid, pivoting spar, with a cloth trailing edge.

Unfortunately, a grooved mast is a pain in the neck since the sail must be extracted from the luff groove when lowering. No one minds on small boats, where the sails are routinely bagged after every sail, but in cruising-size vessels, the main normally lives on its boom, and its luff remains on the track between voyages. Slugs along the luff, running in a recessed track or groove, make a reasonable compromise, allowing some transfer of air but not as much as with the old-fashioned slide-and-track system.

Compared to masts, booms are simple things. They do not have to be streamlined in the same way masts are, and grooving is quite feasible in even the largest of them. A boom plays its part in the game of keeping low and high pressure where they belong. In this case, the air attempts to go under the boom, and

Typical arrangement of slugs in a slotted track along mainsail luff. Note slots on mast and boom, cutback section at main tack for roller reefing.

experiments suggest that the most efficient cross-sectional shape of boom is the flattened tube on its side, providing a barrier that turns back the down-flowing air.

For many years, beginning sailors were taught as an article of faith that the ideal mast was straight and stiff at all times. Many courses still teach this dogma, blithely disregarding the horde of bendy masts and booms on everything from daysailing dinghies to ocean racers.

The sailing world has now divided into the stiff spar and the bendy spar camps. Generally speaking, bendy spars are most commonly seen on smaller boats, but there are enough exceptions so no real hard-and-fast rule is possible. It may help to look at the reasons for each.

Jeremy Howard-Williams, the British sailmaker and writer, has remarked : "A straight mast and boom give the Sail Maker the best chance of cutting a sail which responds accurately to your [the owner's] requirements; he knows what the luff and the foot of the sail will look like when set on your spars. However, you have to pay for this stiffness in weight and windage."*

The weight and windage to which Mr. Howard-Williams refers are caused, of course, by the extra heft of the spar itself and the extra stays and shrouds required to keep the stick straight. As we shall see later on, there are many ways of changing a sail's shape without bending mast or boom. By keeping the mast in a column, the designer maintains control of the stresses involved—which can be enormous, even in a boat of no huge size.

*Jeremy Howard-Williams, *Sails* (Tuckahoe, N.Y.: John de Graff, Inc., 1971) p. 108.

Permanently bent masts have been around for years, as witness this stately cruiser in a Southern California harbor. Fore- and backstays determine the mast's bend.

Edward Brewer has written in this connection that the calculated compression load of one 65-foot mast in a cruiser of his design approached 50,000 pounds. Unless kept under precise control, the failure of a spar under these conditions can be spectacular.

In smaller boats, however, a bendy rig offers quick and reasonably predictable ways of changing the sail shape to suit the wind force of the moment. A mast is designed to bend forward in its center section and aft at the head (which is why the rig is almost always 3/4 or 7/8). Actually, the bend at the masthead is to leeward as well as aft, and both shrouds and forestay tend to slacken somewhat.

The sail responds to the mast's bending by flattening along the luff—an excellent response to a sudden increase in wind speed. The factors acting to bend the mast are fairly complex, and include pressure from the boom, transmitted through the gooseneck; the way in which the mast is secured at deck level (assuming it is stepped on the keel); pressure from the spreaders; jib leech, shroud and backstay tension.

Bendy booms are easier to deal with, and are controlled normally by the sheeting position. Mid-boom sheeting can be used to impose a downward bend, while end-of-the-boom sheeting puts pressure along the leech and allows the boom to curve upward in the center. In the first instance, the downward-curving boom flattens the sail along its foot, while in the second, pulling down on the sheet causes an extra fullness along the foot.

The point to remember in any rig, stiff or bendy, is that the sailmaker must know not only the overall dimensions of the sail he's cutting, but also what shape changes will be imposed by the rig. If you're sailing a standard-class boat, the sailmaker should have a good body of experience to fall back on, but if yours is a one-off or an older boat with new spars, the sailmaker's first try may fall short of perfection.

Standing rigging—the system of wires which holds the mast in place—has undergone a certain amount of change in recent years. For some time after the Marconi rig had become the accepted arrangement for small and medium-size sloops, the standing rigging layout was predictable, with little variation except that dictated by boat size.

The smallest boats had no rigging at all. The mast stepped through the deck into the keel, and required no additional support to hold it up. Slightly larger boats might have a forestay and two shrouds, led up to match the 3/4 or 7/8 rig. Boats up around 20 feet were likely to have a backstay as well—which meant that there had to be a counterbalancing stay to the masthead from the bow. This could be rigged as a straight masthead forestay or by using diamond stays and jumpers, as illustrated.

The point to remember in any rigging situation is that the force applied to one side of the mast must be balanced on the other—either by the strength of the spar itself, which is only practical in small boats, or by stays and shrouds.

Larger sailboats, with more pressures involved, normally had fore- and backstays, upper shrouds led to the masthead, and two pairs of lower shrouds. The upper shrouds led over spreaders—short, round- or oval-sec-

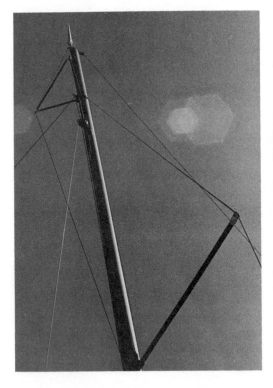

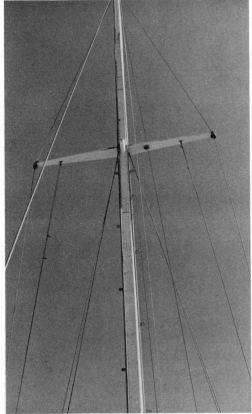

The forestay, leading off down to the left, finishes about a yard below the masthead; to equalize the pull of forestay, upper shrouds and masthead backstay, the diamond shrouds are required. Note how jumper strut bisects the angle of forestay and shrouds.

Wide spreaders on this old-fashioned cruiser's mast give upper shrouds a much better lead to the masthead. Note also the aluminum steps to the crosstrees.

tioned spars apparently at right angles to the mast. Actually, when properly set up, a spreader isn't perpendicular to the mast at all; its outer end is a bit higher than its inner. The theory for many years was that the spreader should bisect the angle made by the shroud, so that the angles made by the spreader and the upper part of the shroud and the spreader and the lower part of the shroud would be the same.

Angles aside, what's important is what the spreader does to the rig. First, it allows the upper shroud to approach the masthead at a greater angle than if it were simply led direct from the chainplates, and this increases the efficiency of the upper shroud. Second, the spreader receives a certain amount of the shroud's load at its outer end and transfers it to the mast—rather as if the spreader were an arrow and the upper shroud the bowstring. In the case of a mast, however, the same bow has two arrows and two strings; when the boat is at rest, the uppers cancel each other out.

But when the boat is under way and heeling, the force on the windward upper shroud is considerably greater than on the leeward one. So much so that the mast would bend

Westerly 28 cruiser has an inner forestay to balance off the pair of aft lowers.

seriously and perhaps even break at the inner end of the spreader were there not additional reinforcement—the lower shroud or shrouds, which have their tangs mounted just under the base of the spreader.

Modern rigs have largely eliminated the forward lower shrouds in favor of a single inner forestay, which serves to make a triangular staying base for the mast, consisting of inner forestay (sometimes called the *babystay*) and port and starboard aft lowers.

There are a good many possible versions of the basic staying system, but they tend to be special cases which can be worked out with a knowledge of the principles of tuning. To see how that works, let's examine the initial setting up of a medium-sized rig—one with masthead fore- and backstays, upper shrouds and single spreaders, aft lowers and a single inner forestay. This is a common and efficient arrangement, a compromise between maximum mast support and minimum windage—and of course everything in boat design is some kind of compromise.

Although serious racers often use solid metal rods for certain kinds of staying jobs, stainless steel wire is still far more common and likely to remain so for the foreseeable future. Stainless is very strong for its weight (see the table of wire strengths in the back of the book) and relatively maintenance-free. It stretches under tension, although not a great deal, and it must therefore have a tension adjustment someplace—usually at deck level, where it's most accessible.

These adjusters, called turnbuckles or (by the British) rigging screws, are also stainless steel, as a rule, though bronze is also used. They can be locked at a given point by pins or rings—a necessity that many people forget, until the turnbuckle backs off and destroys the tuning and perhaps even drops the mast in one's lap.

Most wire standing rigging in use on pleasure craft is of a cross-sectional pattern called *1x19*, which means that the cable is composed of 19 separate strands wound around each other. This arrangement makes the most of the wire's strength, at some sacrifice of flexibility—wire used in running rigging, by contrast, is of a different cross section, called *7x7* or *7x19*, which allows

Three common cross-sections of wire rope: Left to right, 7 x 7 and 7 x 19 semi-flexible for lifts and halyards, 1 x 19 rigid standing rigging.

maximum flex but some loss of strength.

Like rope, the weak point of wire is usually at its end, where it's connected to turnbuckle or tang. Wire must always be led around a curve of greater diameter than equivalent size rope, and wire taken around too sharp a bend will soon begin to break, strand by strand. Stays and shrouds may end in a loop around a thimble, the loop itself secured by an eye splice or by a fitted collar. Alternatively, the wire end may be inserted in a terminal fitting which is literally squeezed to the cable. This latter method forms a very neat, low-friction connection direct to the proper kind of terminal, but it does embody the possibility of sudden disaster. Whereas a failing splice (at least at deck level) is usually visibly bad before it lets go, a terminal socket may be quietly and invisibly corroding inside itself with no one the wiser.

Such failures are, I should emphasize, quite rare, and there's not a great deal of point in brooding about them. The only practical precaution is periodic inspection of the end fittings for rust, which indicates that the stainless has perished.

The first step in tuning a mast is to make sure the spar itself is correctly seated in its step, with the base of the mast flush against the plate of the step. Since compression loads on the spar are very great at the base, it's especially important to take the time to ensure that there's as much area of the mast foot as possible in contact with the step. This is even more vital when the mast is deck-stepped, without support from mast partners.

Now attach the upper shrouds and stays and take them up tight enough so the spar is straight and doesn't wobble. At this point the people and/or machinery that have got the mast up to vertical can relax and let go. Make fast the lower shrouds and inner forestay and take up those turnbuckles just enough so you can check the lead of the wire and turnbuckle. This, too, is an important precaution and one that's all too frequently ignored in the bustle of getting the mast up and the boat away from

Built-in toggle on this shroud turnbuckle keeps the lead to chainplate fair. Unlike older patterns, this turnbuckle can be adjusted with a wrench and locks with nuts.

the rigging crane.

If the lead from the tang on the mast down the stay and turnbuckle to the chainplate on deck isn't straight, the rig may well fail at some later point. It's not easy to mold in a chainplate with exactly the proper angle for a straight lead to the masthead, and if your stay's lead has a bend in it, by all means insert a toggle if the manufacturer hasn't already done so.

In many cases, the designer of your boat will have specified a degree of rake normal to the tuned mast—it should be noted on the sailplan drawing, at the masthead. Approximate this as best you can—a right triangle formed by the mast, cabin top and a weighted line dropped from the masthead should be not too hard to calculate.

Now take the upper shroud turnbuckles tight, carefully sighting up the mast to make sure it remains straight. How tight is tight? There is no absolute answer, which is why tuning is an art, not a science. If you can tweak the shrouds on an already-tuned boat of comparable size and rig, that at least will give you a feel for the degree of tautness. In any case, it is better at first to err on the side of slackness.

Having attended to the upper shrouds, take up the fore- and backstays in the same way, being careful not to alter the preset mast rake as you do so. These stays should at first be approximately as taut as the upper shrouds.

Set up the inner forestay next, not as taut as the masthead forestay. For starters, the inner stay should have all appreciable slack taken out—you may want to take it up more later, but this will depend to a certain extent on the cut of your mainsail. If your boat has forward lower shrouds instead of an inner forestay, take them up equally to just about this same amount of tension.

The aft lower shrouds should normally be the least taut of all, a prescription as hard to define as very tight. To begin with, try setting them so there is no visible flap of loose wire,

a

Rigging expert Don Posey tunes a
Hirondelle cruising cat at Marina Del Rey
in California. With fore- and backstays and
upper shrouds taken up initially, he checks
mast alignment, sighting along recessed
track.

Twin forestays must be equally taut.
Without a tension meter, touch is perhaps
the most reliable method, as shown here.

b

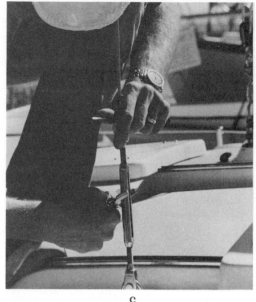

c

When tightening a standard turnbuckle, it's
important to immobilize the upper screw
while turning the barrel to avoid
transmitting the turns to the wire.

Don can just reach the aft lowers on either
side to check one against the other. They
and the corresponding inner forestay
should be fairly slack at rest.

d

but a perceptible slackness to the touch. Pin all the turnbuckles, but if you use standard cotter pins, don't open them more than the bare amount necessary to hold them in place. (Obviously you will have permanently pinned the top and bottom points of each turnbuckle, to wire terminal and chainplate. There is no adjustment to allow for at the ends.)

This is just the beginning of tuning. Under tension, the wire will stretch even if you don't sail the boat, so the upper shrouds and stays will have to be taken up a bit anyway after a day or so. And the really serious business of tuning under sail remains to be done.

If possible (and it seldom is, of course), try to tune your rig on a day when the wind strength is perhaps a bit more than the average velocity for your area, but not so much that you can't concentrate on what you're doing. Recheck to make absolutely sure the mast is vertical and has no bends in it. Sight up the mast groove or track first, then stand off on the dock or on another boat to ascertain if the mast is straight in the boat—something that's very hard to determine from your own deck.

Hoist your main and working jib (or whatever serves as your most usual headsail—in light-air areas, it may be the #1 genoa) and sail to a place where you have room to reach, beat and run for several minutes without changing course. Your crew should consist of at least two other people: one to steer and one to handle the sheets. With untaped pins in the turnbuckles, your sheet hand must be very gentle tacking and trimming, to avoid snags.

Put the boat on either tack, close-hauled. When she has settled down and is moving well, sight up the mast to check the thwartships alignment. If the spar is sagging off to leeward at the head, while the lower part seems straight, the upper shroud is probably too slack. But if the whole spar seems to bow to windward in the middle, then the lower shroud (or both lowers) may be too taut.

Underway, sight up the mast on alternate tacks to check for: (A) slack upper shroud, (B) slack windward lower shroud; mast should be straight, as in (C) on either tack. When you've finished tuning underway, re-check rig to make sure spar is straight at rest.

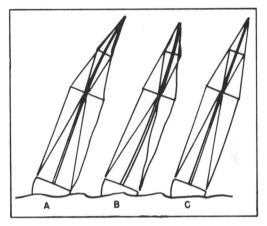

On the other hand, if the masthead is hooked to windward, the lower or lowers are too slack. Take up or loosen just as much as required to get the spar straight for whatever tack you're on. Now go over to the other tack and repeat the process. It may take several attempts before the spar is suitably vertical.

Next check the fore-and-aft alignment. Probably the most common problem is a sag-

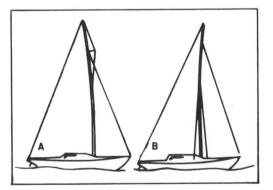

The backstay is frequently the key to fore and aft tuning. Jumpers, as in (A), cannot usually be adjusted. In (B), backstay is probably too slack.

With twin forestays, it's easy to get an exaggerated picture of sag under load.

ging headstay—if yours is drooping down to leeward without a bend in the mast, then luff up, drop the jib, and take up on the forestay turnbuckle. If, on the other hand, the stay is sagging and there is a forward hook at the top of the mast, take up on the backstay. Have a good look at the mainsail—with substantial tension on downhaul and foot it should have assumed a fairly flat curve, no belly along the luff. If this is not the case, try tightening the inner forestay, even putting a slight forward bow in the middle of the mast.

With the sail shapes adequate for main and big jib on a beat, try the boat reaching and running. You should be able to make the sails assume a good shape without adjustments to the standing rigging, unless yours is a type of boat in which the backstay is meant to be adjusted under way. In that case you'll have to experiment with the proper amount to slack off on the backstay when off the wind. Some suggestions are included in the appropriate chapters in Part II.

Spars and standing rigging are specified by your boat's designer. Generally speaking, if there's something wrong, something that cannot be adjusted out, it's fair to assume that you, the owner, are at fault. Not always, however: a boat and its rig may be built and assembled by several different groups of people, and problems of detail may develop from lack of communication among them. For instance, it is not unknown for stays to be too long or too short for proper adjustment. Small alterations can be made with toggles or different size turnbuckles, but if in doubt, check with the builder or designer.

Running rigging is much more the owner's decision, even where certain items are supplied by the builder. Tastes and requirements in gear vary, but the following suggestions may be helpful.

Halyards: On small boats, halyards are normally Dacron rope. On larger craft, main and jib halyards are wire line with Dacron tails, and spinnaker and staysail halyards are Dacron. (As a rule of thumb, stretchy nylon sails take rope halyards, less stretchy Dacron sails take wire).

The problem is in the intermediate size of boat: At what point do wire halyards become a must? There is no hard-and-fast answer, but if you can get good tension on the luff of main and jib *and maintain it through a couple of hours hard on the wind*, then whatever halyard you're using is adequate. But if, having sweated the sail up to a nice, taut luff, you find it becoming scalloped along the leading edge after a half-hour beat, something's wrong. Either you didn't get the luff tight enough in the first place, or your boom downhaul (if the problem's in the main) is slipping, or the rope halyard is stretching. The remedy for the last is wire—*but* remember to check that the halyard sheave is of a sufficiently large diameter so that the wire strands don't break. Manufacturers have precalculated the correct diameters, but if you're switching from a rope to a wire halyard, you may also have to change the halyard sheave.

The wire part of the halyard (assuming it has a rope tail) will be long enough to run from the masthead, when the sail is raised, down to the winch and around it four or five times. The rope tail should be hitched to the halyard cleat. Obviously it's impossible to do this for several sizes of jib, and the answer is simply to add a removable wire extension at the head of smaller jibs, to get the wire down to the winch.

And what about halyard winches? The racing boats featured in yachting magazines seldom have less than a thousand dollars worth of winches just for the halyards alone, but few of us require anything so elaborate. For mainsails under about 200 square feet, a winch probably isn't necessary at all, as long as you have a power-of-two downhaul tackle (or better) at the gooseneck. Beyond that size, or lacking a sliding gooseneck, an ordinary drum winch is usually quite adequate at least in boats of 30 feet or so.

Jibs, on the other hand, are more difficult to tension sufficiently, and their luffs require tension more than do mainsails, anyway. Like mains, jibs develop a good deal of friction along the luff as they're raised, and it is hard to get enough tension down toward the foot of the sail. In addition, the jib normally doesn't have room for a tack downhaul (although under-deck tack tackles seem to be coming into favor among the hot racers). So wire halyard and a winch will often be necessary for a fairly small jib.

Except in very large boats, sheets are almost always Dacron, not wire. Although even prestretched Dacron stretches more than a little, sheets are seldom cleated for great lengths of time, and can be much more easily adjusted than can halyards. The question of what size sheets—or how many sizes—and whether laid or braided construction is one which really requires a personal answer. My own recommendations for a sloop between 16 and 20 feet would consist of one set of 5/16" or 3/8" Dacron sheets usable for all jibs and the spinnaker, and (if you sail in waters where light airs are a fact of life) an additional pair of ghosting sheets of 1/8" flag halyard braid. The standard sheets really need only be 1/4" in diameter* for strength, but the average person's hand simply doesn't fit quarter-inch line comfortably, and if you're going to be hauling and easing such a line all afternoon, you want something you can get a good grip on. In addition, extra thickness does give extra protection from chafe. Braided line for sheets is certainly the fashionable thing, but I have my doubts how much easier it is to the hand. There doesn't seem to be any great difference to me—but other more experienced skippers feel quite the opposite. In the cockpit of a small boat, it does help if the mainsheet and the jib and/or spinnaker sheets are easy to tell apart. Color coding helps, to be sure, but so does having different construction and diameter. In this latter connection, it's surprising how easily one can distinguish between two lines 1/16" different in size, after a bit of experience.

And finally, if there is any need to splice the lines (with sheets there usually isn't), laid line is a lot easier to splice than braid.

4. Variant Rigs

Not all boats, thank heaven, are sloops —what a paralyzingly dull prospect that would be. There are less elaborate spar and sail systems, and far more complex ones, and there's a reason—if not the right one—to

---

*All lines are referred to by diameter. In commercial usage and in some foreign countries, rope sizes are often given in circumference, which of course yields much larger figures for the same size line: circumference = 3.14 x diameter.

choose each. Let's look at the more common ones and what they do. The definitions —despite nautical dictionaries—are somewhat fluid, and in certain cases I have used terms that seem more meaningful than the traditional ones, or definitions that seem to me to describe the real difference between one rig and another.

One mast, one sail

There are a number of genuine variations on this simplest of themes. One of the most popular is the lateen, a triangular sail set from a yard hoisted to the masthead. The sail's foot may or may not have a boom—if it does, the boom is joined at its forward end to the yard's lower end. One halyard, one sheet, and few worthwhile complications. This is of course the standard rig on boardboats, popularized by the Sailfish and Sunfish. Unlike other single-sail rigs, the lateen is partially balanced, carrying a certain proportion of its sail area forward of the mast.

It's not a particularly efficient rig to windward, but with a light, flat-bottomed sailing surfboard it works well enough to provide an exciting ride. The low-cost sail neither needs nor can use the multiple adjustments common to more sophisticated rigs. Simple and inexpensive, the lateen is better off the wind than some of its relatives, because it doesn't develop the killing weather helm common to many one sail arrangements. The lateen-rigged sailboard is not a particularly kindly boat for the beginning sailor (except in the pocketbook), because things go wrong so fast that there's seldom time to tell what you did before you're swimming. On the other hand, the boat is easy to get back on its feet and sail off, and tipping over is certainly a direct suggestion that you weren't handling the boat

correctly.

Una rig is a term more common across the water than here, and refers to a boat with a single Marconi or Bermudan sail, usually of sophisticated design, with a bendy, and often pivoting, mast and vanging arrangement. The Finn is perhaps the archetype of the una, and the Laser one of its recent versions. These are still small boats, but they offer one or two people good performance.

Catboats are hard to define. Any boat with a single mast and sail can be said to be cat-rigged, but I think it more informative to save the term for the traditional American catboat—shallow, often gaff-rigged, with an immense barn door rudder on the transom, a huge centerboard, and a beam usually about half the boat's length.

The gaff rig, which appears nowadays more

This 17-foot gaff-rigged catboat by Jay Benford has a hull made of ferro-cement.

often on catboats than anywhere else, is a frank archaism. It is heavier than a Marconi rig (and the weight is up high, where it helps least), far more complex, and a flop to windward. It is, to a great many people, fun to look at and fun to sail. A gaff-rigged hull would probably be faster off the wind than the same hull Marconi-rigged; but. that's a false comparison, by and large, because there are so few Marconi catboats.

Similar to the gaff rig is the *sliding gunter* seen mostly on sailing prams. About the only functional difference is that here the gaff is so arranged that it lies parallel to the mast and extends it upward. The reason for this complexity is that in very small boats at anchor, a tall mast can frequently lead to uncontrolled rolling, followed by capsize. The lower gunter (or lateen) spar minimizes weight aloft when the boat has no counterbalancing crew weight in the cockpit. Under way, the gunter rig performs much like a Marconi main, but slightly less efficiently to windward.

One mast, multiple sails

The sloop, of course. Today, most people who think about it consider the sloop to be a single-masted boat with two working sails, one forward of the spar, one aft. That's a serviceable definition, although it begs the question of what is a *working sail* these days. My own definition would be somewhat broader: a sloop is a one-masted sailboat capable of setting a mainsail and one or more headsails simultaneously.

Readers will object that this definition effectively scuttles the cutter. So it does, but only because the term *cutter* has no modern usage, except when someone appears with an antique boat. The double-headsail sloop has

eaten up the cutter, like it or not.

But what about sloops with multiple headsails? For the most part, jib and staysail (the headsail set to the inner forestay) are a combination designed, yet again, to work around that part of the racing handicap measurement which restricts sail area forward of the mast. Rather than being intended to reduce the jib area to two manageable segments, the modern double headsail is designed so that an additional staysail can be carried in addition to an oversize jib.

There are, however, a few boats being designed with a modern version of the traditional double headsail rig, in which the staysail is self-tending (that is, set on a boom like the main) and the high-clewed jib is cut to

A modern double headsail rig, as opposed to the traditional style, on an Ericson 25, designed by Bruce King. She is more usually rigged as a masthead sloop.

The Drascombe Driver from England has a most unusual rig—a lug mainsail without a boom and a mizzen that sheets to a boomkin. Ketch or yawl—you choose.

stay out of the staysail's way as much as possible. For the cruising man, there is a lot to be said for a rig which can be short-tacked single handed—and which can alternatively carry the masses of sail required to push a heavy boat in light airs or when there's a crowd of willing guests aboard.

Two masts

Ketch, yawl and schooner are options that traditionally attract the shorthanded cruising skipper with a big boat. Actually there is nothing morally repugnant about a 24-foot ketch or schooner. It won't sail as efficiently as a sloop of the same size, but so what? If you enjoy it, that's all that counts.

Uffa Fox once wrote that the largest size sail which could be handled by a single sailor was one of approximately 500 square feet. In late middle age, Sir Francis Chichester felt that 300 square feet per sail was more appropriate for him, single-handing in the open ocean. Certainly those two figures are both reasonable. When it comes time to split the rig into smaller triangles, one has the choice of several sails forward of the mast or of spreading the entire rig lower and longer in the boat.

Like the sloop and the cutter, the ketch and the yawl are becoming less distinguishable from each other. Not long ago, the yawl was simply a sloop with a small balancing mast aft of the rudder post, while the ketch was a genuine, two-masted rig in which the sail area of the fore-triangle plus the mizzen was more or less the same as that of the main, and the mizzen was at least one-third the area of the main. The mizzenmast was stepped forward of the rudder post.

With the revival of transom hung rudders, the shortening of main booms, and the continuing exploration among ocean racers for loopholes in the sail area rules, there has arisen a curious vehicle which might best be called the racing ketch. It's a ketch by virtue of having its rudder post at the transom so any mast is forward of it, but the two masts are virtually independent of each other, and the mizzen is largely removed from the dirty air of the main (one of the curses of ketch performance).

The true yawl has largely declined in popularity, while the old-fashioned ketch seems to be staging something of a comeback. That's because the yawl was serviceable as long as rating rules favored it, but it was never the genuine, two-sticker that would be useful to a cruising man. The true ketch is not much good to windward compared to a sloop, but it is a very easy boat to sail, especially shorthanded.

Both ketch and, to a lesser extent, yawl offer the advantage and extra cost of many possible combinations of sail to suit varying wind conditions. Ketch skippers are fond of referring to how well their craft sail under jib and mizzen, but many ketches do far better by simply striking the mizzen entirely when the wind pipes up.

If one is interested in preserving reasonable windward sailing efficiency, there is not much point in considering a two-stick rig in boats of less than 35-40 feet, with a conventional, old-style keel. If one simply wants a two-masted boat, just about any size is fine.

What of the schooner? Like the gaff rig, the schooner is an attractive antique. Like the gaff, the schooner is an acquired taste, and probably one which should not be sampled too early in a sailing life. A schooner is perhaps even easier than a ketch to sail alone, having its largest sail reachable from the cockpit, but it is a dog to windward, and the mainmast in the center of the cabin can be something of a problem when planning the accommodation.

My own feeling, having owned ketch, catboat and sloop, Marconi and gaff rigs, is that gaffs are great to look at on someone else's vessel; that catboats are marvelous for poking about harbors; and that ketches are fine as long as they have nice, large engines for going to windward. One opinion, to be sure, but at least undisguised. I have not yet tried a yawl but would certainly consider it, if only to have once again the use of a mizzen staysail (of which more later), one of the greatest sails devised by man.

5. Balance and Steering

A sailboat's balance under way is crucial to her efficient performance, yet balance is one of the most difficult subjects to grapple with. The helmsman fighting a hard-mouthed boat has a very clear picture of what balance means, and so does the designer brooding about how much lead to allow between CE and CLR. The trouble is that both these people are operating in quite different worlds.

A few definitions may help to pin down the problem and suggest just how much gap exists between theory and practicality.

C. A. Marchaj, normally a writer of numbing technicality, defines *balance* simply as "satisfactory directional stability," "the property of needing little helm to maintain a given straight course, whatever the boat's sailing attitude, conditions, or speed."*

Note, in passing, that Marchaj says *little* helm, not *no* helm. There's a considerable difference, as we shall see.

Lee and *weather helm* are also relative properties of a boat. Respectively, they refer to a boat's tendency to swing to leeward or to

*C. A. Marchaj, *Sailing Theory and Practice* (New York: Dodd, Mead Co., 1964) p. 350.

weather when the tiller is released. As it happens, of course, lee and weather helm increase and decrease according to a number of factors besides the boat's theoretical balance—factors including, but not limited to, her fore and aft trim, the heading relative to the wind, the amount of heel and wind strength. It is possible (if not very ordinary) for a boat to have weather helm under some circumstances and lee helm under others.

Generally speaking, lee helm is considered undesirable across the board. The most obvious reason cited has been safety. If you let go of the tiller and your boat falls off into an uncontrolled jibe, sooner or later you're likely to get into trouble.

Second, since most helmsmen and nearly all helmswomen find it more comfortable to pull against a tiller than to push it, and since most steering is done from the windward side of the cockpit, it can be very tiring to have to handle a tiller with lee helm for any length of time.

Finally, and perhaps most important, a boat with lee helm is getting no fin advantage from her rudder when working to windward. More on that later.

When discussing weather helm, most authorities agree that a slight degree of it is a good thing. For a wonder, most of them also agree more or less on what "slight" means —the rudder at an angle of 2° to 4° from the boat's centerline. More than 5° is definitely a drag, on the hull and on the helmsman.

Why should weather helm be good? The reasons are largely the reverse of why lee helm is bad. A weather-helmed boat will luff up into the wind if the tiller is free; steering from the windward side of the cockpit is not especially tiring, and the slight angle of rudder gives a positive feel to the tiller; and finally, when the rudder is cocked at a slight angle to the keel as in the diagram of a boat with weather helm, it acts to contribute a certain amount of lift to windward.

36

Comes now the conflict of theory and reality. When a designer creates a boat, he deals with two basic concepts that have great effect on the sail plan and the underwater shape. These are the Center of Effort (normally abbreviated CE) and the Center of Lateral Plane (CLP; sometimes called Center of Lateral Resistance, or CLR).

The first of these terms refers to the geometrical center of the boat's sail plan, a point noted on most designers' drawings as a small double circle slightly aft or slightly forward of the mast. This point is easy to figure for most boats, in the following fashion:

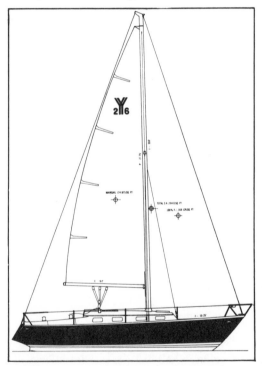

Sail plan for the Sparkman & Stephens-designed Yankee 26 shows the standard dimensional abbreviations. CE is just forward of the mast and inside the babystay.

First, on a copy of the full sail plan determine the geometrical center of the mainsail by drawing a straight line from the head of the sail to a point halfway

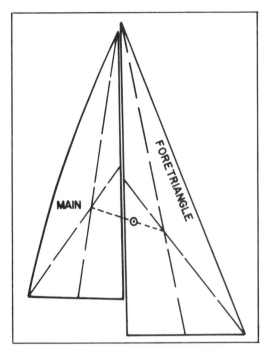

How to derive the CE of main, foretriangle and sailplan. For individual sail, draw a straight line from the center of one edge to the corner of the opposite angle, then repeat with another edge; intersection is CE of that sail. Draw a line connecting these two points and divide it proportionally according to the sails' areas; the division point is the CE of the whole.

along the foot. Now draw a second line from the clew to a point halfway up the luff. The intersection is the CE of the main.

Second, find the CE of the foretriangle in the same way. If your boat's standard jib doesn't fill the foretriangle, use its actual shape.

Third, connect the two CEs by a straight line, and measure the length of it, using the same scale as the sail plan. Divide the line approximately in two parts, the parts being proportional to the areas of the two sails. The CE of the total sail plan will of course lie closer to or on the larger sail.

It's possible to fix the theoretical CE with

great precision, but there isn't a great deal of point to it. The true Center of Effort would have to take into account the mainsail's roach as well as any curve in the jib leech, both of which are ignored by this formula. In any case, under sailing conditions the CE moves forward and aft.

The Center of Lateral Plane is even easier to determine and requires no math at all. Just trace the underwater profile of your boat on a piece of paper, mount it on light cardboard, and cut it out. Balance the cutout on the point of a pin. The balance point is the CLP.

Having determined both CE and CLP, and having noted them on the sail and hull profile, you can measure the horizontal distance between the two, which is called the *lead*. In a well-designed boat, the CE will always be slightly forward of the CLP—anywhere from 5 to 20 percent of the waterline length, according to naval architects.

The reasons for this have to do with the designer's recognition that both CE and CLP as drawn are not only fictional but also subject to change in the real, moving boat. CE is drawn as if the sails were strapped flat in. As sheets are eased, the sails become fuller and move forward and to leeward, moving the true, or aerodynamic, CE forward. In the same way, the CLP changes in a moving boat, and the real balance of a boat is very hard to calculate on paper—if it weren't, there would

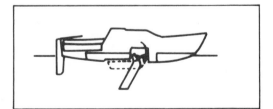

CLR of this swing-keel vessel changes as the keel moves forward and aft as well as being raised and lowered. On a centerboard boat, adjustment of the board is infinite, but a swing keel is normally either all the way up or down and locked.

be far less need for in-the-water tuning.

On a keel sailboat, there's not a great deal the average owner can do about adjusting the CLP, but a boat with a changeable underbody—be it centerboard, daggerboard or even leeboard—can be rebalanced under way both above and below the water. As most people recall, centerboards and pivoting leeboards (the old, or Dutch, style) not only swing up and down, but also forward and aft, while daggerboards slide either vertically or at a slight angle that has the effect of moving the board's area forward as it is raised.

If, after a few sails in assorted weather conditions, you feel that your boat isn't well balanced—that she has lee helm, a completely neutral helm, or a weather helm that angles the rudder more than about 5° to the centerline, there are several steps you can take before consulting the designer or the boat yard.

These days, weather helm is a far more common problem than lee helm, so we'll deal with it first.

If you have a centerboard boat, try sailing with the board further up than usual. Raising the board of course moves its area aft, and with it the CLR.

Retune the rig so that the mast is raked less aft. Even a bit of forward rake is permissible.

Try sailing with the main flatter but less strapped in (see comments on mainsail adjustment in the next chapter).

Try a larger jib, if possible.

If none of these works, you'll probably have to resort to more heroic measures—and it's worth the extra cost to discuss the problem with the boat's designer, if he's available, or with another architect before doing anything structural.

Essentially what you want to do is increase the lead by moving the CE forward, since it's impractical to move the CLR aft. You can do this by having your sailmaker recut the main to shorten the foot. You can also attempt to

increase the length of the foretriangle, by adding a short bowsprit. If the boat isn't too large, you may be able to move the mast step forward without a major reconstruction.

The solutions to lee helm are largely the reverse of the suggestions above. You're attempting to move the CE aft and closer to the CLR, and you can do it by raking the mast more sharply, moving the jib tack aft, lowering the centerboard, using a larger main or a smaller jib.

My own feeling is that if the boat remains unsatisfactory after minor alteration, you may be best advised to sell it. You'll probably take a loss, but it won't be nearly as much money as you could spend trying to redesign the boat piecemeal.

Assuming that the boat's balance is adequate, it may be worth spending a little time examining the steering system. As noted above, a sailboat's rudder—unlike that of a power boat—serves both to control direction and to supply lift to windward. Together with the keel or centerboard, it is a fin, but unlike them its angle of attack can be changed.

As with any part of the boat that's underwater, the rudder is also a source of frictional drag. The amount of drag depends on the

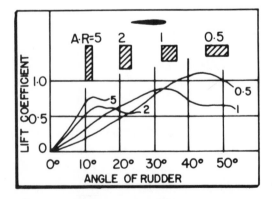

Lift provided by various aspect ratios of rudder at different angles. Note that high aspect ratio provides good lift at low angle, as opposed to "barn door" style. (After E. S. Brewer)

38

shape, the area and the angle at which the rudder meets the oncoming stream of water. Today's consensus is that high-aspect ratio rudders are definitely preferable in the windward phase of sailing. A rudder with an aspect ratio of around 4:1 provides far better lift and considerably less drag than a rudder with the same area but less aspect ratio, when sailing with 3° of weather helm.*

But, as always, there are disadvantages to balance off the good qualities. The high aspect ratio rudder stalls out easily—that is, it loses lift quickly and adds drag if turned sharply and/or too far. In any steering, helmsmen should lead into a turn with a relatively shallow rudder angle, and then add helm as the boat begins to swing. This technique is even more important when using the high-efficiency lever of a modern spade rudder placed well aft and separated from keel or centerboard.

The best kind of rudder—all other things being equal, as they seldom or never are—is one hung behind a narrow, protective skeg, which adds balance to the rudder itself. Instead of the half-heart profile common to older rudders, a straight trailing edge is now preferred, at right angles to the straight foot of the rudder. In cross section, a rudder blade should be rounded at its forward edge, tapering to a sharp after edge, with the maximum thickness about a third of the distance back.

One refinement seen more and more often is the transom-hung rudder that rides up and down in a frame, so that the blade depth can be adjusted as required. Unlike the kick-up rudder seen on off-the-beach sailboats, the lifting rudder is unprotected against damage, and a grounding at speed is likely to destroy both frame and blade. But the ability to lift underwater appendages can perceptibly increase speed under many conditions, besides

*Edward Brewer, in *Sail* magazine. April, 1972, page 81, "Performance as a Function of Hull Design: Rudders".

making for a surface easier to keep smooth and clean, and a boat that can take the ground more easily.

6. Sails Today

Almost everything about today's sails is conditioned by racing and its special requirements; size, shape, cut, material, adjustability—you name the factor, and chances are that racing has structured it. Cruising people grumble about this situation a good deal, conveniently disregarding the fact that were it not for racing, sail construction would probably still be back at flax edged with leather. True, racing requirements have in some areas stalled sail development, and the person who feels he has been cheated out of usable area or a helpful sail shape is free to press ahead on his own. The problem is that he'll be a real groundbreaker, with little commercial assistance.

Because racing is so important, it is very helpful for any sailor to be able to read and understand the sail plans of commercially produced sailboats. There's a lot of information available in these plans, but the terms used are somewhat special, and don't always mean what simple English would suggest.

Start by examining the sail plan of a standard sloop, shown in profile view. The amount of information provided by the designer varies—usually according to the performance index of the boat: That is, a boat which has race-winning potential is going to get a lot of attention from readers who are likely to want detailed information; a boat obviously destined for pottering around is likely to be sailed by skippers who don't care much about the precise size of her sails.

The bare minimum usually shown is the square footage of main and foretriangle, the total sail area, and the CEs of each sail and of the total sail plan. Bear in mind, however,

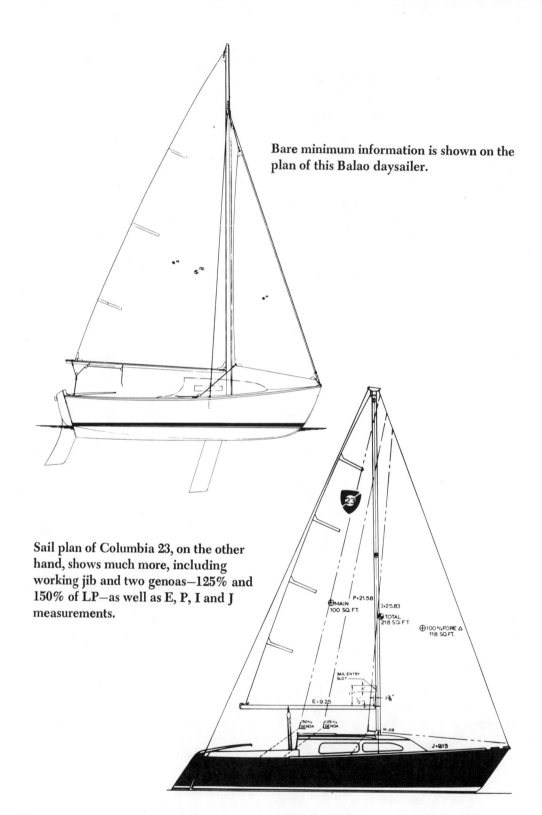

Bare minimum information is shown on the plan of this Balao daysailer.

Sail plan of Columbia 23, on the other hand, shows much more, including working jib and two genoas—125% and 150% of LP—as well as E, P, I and J measurements.

P=21.58

⊕MAIN
100 SQ.FT.

I=25.83

⊕TOTAL
218 SQ.FT.

⊕100%FORE △
118 SQ.FT.

SAIL ENTRY
SLOT

E=9.25

150%
GENOA

125%
GENOA

W.JIB

J=8.15

that the sail area of the main is actually larger than what is shown on the sail plan, because in measuring, the mainsail is assumed to be a right triangle, and the roach is "free," or unmeasured, area. Although a jib—often a large genoa—may be drawn into the profile view, the foretriangle square footage is what is shown on the sail plan.

There may also, on all but the most basic sail plans, be four other measurements shown, each coded by a single letter: E and P for the main, and I and J for the foretriangle. E is the length of the mainsail foot, P is the maximum length of the mainsail hoist from the upper edge of the boom to the top of the headboard. The "official" mainsail area, thus, comes out to (ExP)÷2.

The measurement for I is considerably longer than P. Measured down the forward side of the mast, I normally runs from the intersection of the mast and the highest stay on which a sail is set, down to a point approximately at deck level. For practical purposes, it is the height of the mast from the deck. J is the horizontal distance between the forward side of the mast (or its extension downward) to the point where the forestay cuts the rail cap. I and J are another right angle, and so the listed area of the foretriangle is (IxJ(÷2.

In actual measuring, it is fair to say, the formula is a lot more complicated. Readers interested in being swamped by formulae derived from sophistical measurements of minute details can find it all in Peter Johnson's book *Yachtsman's Guide to the Rating Rule* (Chicago: Quadrangle Books, 1971).

One more measurement is frequently bandied about, and it is one that's frequently misunderstood. *LP*, which stands for Luff Perpendicular, refers to the line drawn perpendicular to the forestay and taken back to the clew of the largest headsail. Obviously, each headsail on a boat has a different LP, but when a sailboat is being measured for a handicap rating, it is only the greatest LP that counts. Today, except where one-design rules dictate otherwise, the standard LP is 150% of the J measurement. Many people have got it into their heads that the foot of the largest genoa is 150% of J. Not so.

Because of the ingenuity of man, and especially that breed of man which races sailboats, almost every measurement of a sail is controlled by one racing authority or another. What's irritating for the nonracer, however, is the degree to which this control extends to boats that were never seriously intended to race. The talented people who design boats and cut sails are so imbued with the racing rule they live under that they seldom think of attempting any innovation that cannot be conformed to the rule.

The fully battened sail is one such idea. It has been tried on monohulls as well as on multihulls, and for cruising boats it offers a good many potential advantages: A fully battened main can be shaped to maximum advantage easily; it is unlikely to luff itself to pieces; it reefs easily. But the length of battens (as well as their number) is regulated; so except in multihulls and among the very strong-minded, there is little reason to experiment.

Sails today are, however, miraculous contrivances compared with what has gone before. At this writing, we seem to be on the verge of another step forward in sail material but for the foreseeable future, the sails used by all except the most high-powered racers seem likely to remain more or less as they are.

Sails are made of nylon or Dacron, depending on what is required of them—Dacron for mains and jibs, where maintenance of the correct shape requires a low-stretch fabric, and nylon for light-weather headsails and other ancillary sails where extreme light weight is demanded and stretchiness is no drawback. Nylon is sometimes used as well in the inexpensive sails supplied with mass-produced small craft, and in this application the sails' small area means that the nylon will not have too much chance to pull out of shape.

Almost all Dacron sails are so strong that, accidents aside, they will continue to exist far beyond the point where they're good sails. The best Dacron sails are made with a high thread count and a low proportion of filler; that is, there are more filaments to the square inch, making a tighter sail more capable of retaining its designed shape. Filler, which is bonded right into the sail fabric, will make a cheap sail look good for a while, but after prolonged use—maybe as little as a year—the finish will start to crack and the sail to bag.

Fortunately for the boat owner, in dealing with the sailmaking industry, he is working with a group of people who really care what they're doing and who will extend themselves beyond the normal call of duty as a regular thing. Sailmaking is one of the last real service professions, and the relationship between a knowledgeable owner and his sailmaker is a very complex, two-way affair.

The question of which sails to own at a given stage in one's sailing career has received a lot of attention, proving only that there are a great many possible answers. Before offering my own prescription, I would like to suggest what the variables seem to me to be. First, of course, is the kind of boat. If you have a daysailing catboat, you need one sail. Period. If your class association restricts your sail wardrobe, then you get what everyone else gets.

But if you have a choice, then you will have to consider the boat's capabilities, the kind of weather in which you sail, the crew you usually have available, and how much you have to spend. The small daysailing sloop cannot normally make use of more than four sails at the most—at least not until her owner is fairly well up in serious competition. These basic sails—a term more useful, I think, than working sails, the canvas under which a sailboat

42

fished or lugged goods—are the main, jib, genoa and spinnaker. As a rule, there is not a great deal of choice to be made in the cut or style of each. Go to a sailmaker who cuts for the better sailors in your class, and take his advice about cloth weight and the like.

If the sailmaker sails in your class himself, so much the better. The only time when your opinion—at this stage—may be worth inflicting on a sailmaker is when he works and sails on waters where wind conditions are quite different from where you are. Look up the average wind speeds for your area over the sailing months (they're in the *Coast Pilot*) and average them out. It can make a difference.

On the small cruising boat there will be more decisions for you to make. When selecting a mainsail, get one with as many possible adjustment features as you can. Even if you can't take advantage of them now, you'll want them soon enough. Be sure the sailmaker knows the track system of your spars and the kind of reefing you have. Your main should have some kind of outhaul arrangement to tension the foot, even if you have to rig it yourself. You should consider the addition of a zipper foot on the main—nothing more than a device to make the mainsail fuller off the wind and in light airs. A leech line is another good idea serving much the same purpose.

Your first headsails pose another problem. The old working jib is largely passé these days. It was a sail that filled the foretriangle and was the jib normally used under most sailing conditions. Today's sailor hooks on his number 1 genoa as the standard thing—if you want to call one sail the working jib, that's it. This genoa will be at least 150% LP, and possibly as much as 170 or 180. The exact size depends on how much you intend to race. If you're not a racer, I'd say go for the 180 for sure, unless your boat is exceptionally tender.

For heavy weather conditions, a type of jib called the *lapper* has appeared to supersede the working jib in this area. The lapper is

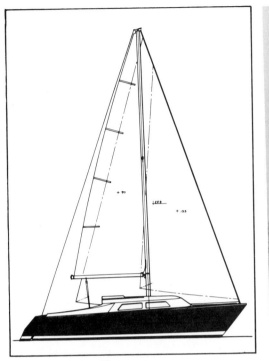

The normal extremes of headsail size are the lapper and 180% genoa shown on the plan of this Ray Hunt-designed Paceship 23.

A standard-cut all purpose spinnaker being carried on a reach by this Ranger 23. A starcut might be more effective on this heading, but would be less generally useful.

generally a sail with the approximate area of a working jib—about equal to the foretriangle—but with a shorter luff and a longer foot. The theory is simple enough: in heavy weather, sail area high up tends to heel the boat more than drive it; so the same square footage is transplanted down along the deck.

The only drawback to the lapper is the fact that it *does* overlap the mast, often just enough so that in windy weather the hand at the jib halyard is repeatedly slugged by the jib clew and whatever sheet attachment you've placed there. (Another good reason, parenthetically, for securing jib sheets with a bowline. If you've ever been popped across the bridge of the nose by a stainless steel snapshackle, you're not likely to forget it. A knot is considerably softer.)

The fourth essential sail is an all-purpose spinnaker. At least one authority recommends a star-cut reaching chute as the first spinnaker, but I cannot go along with that. Your big genoa will be your close-reaching sail, at least for a while, and the spinnaker will better serve its natural function as a downwind addition. But as to the need for a chute, there's no question in my mind. The spinnaker is not only a marvelous sail in itself, but it's also virtually required equipment on any modern design with a large foretriangle and a small main.

When your finances have recovered somewhat from this sail-buying binge, you will have to consider your next move. If you sail in waters where the wind comes on strong frequently, you'll probably want to get a storm jib next. This small, heavy sail will usually require a wire extension from the tack to the deck fitting to prevent it from being filled by waves over the bow. An additional extension for a wire halyard at the head of the sail may also be necessary.

43

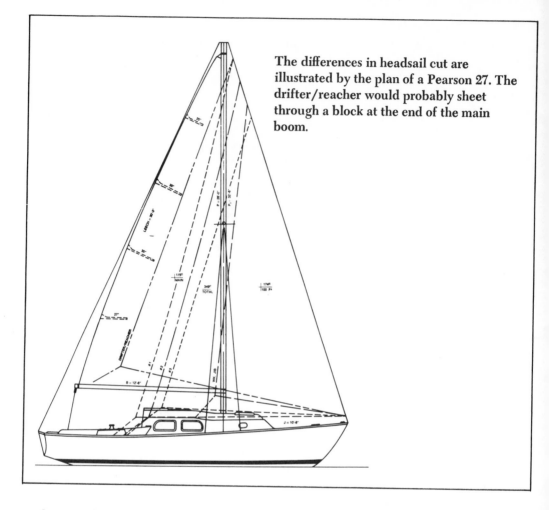

The differences in headsail cut are illustrated by the plan of a Pearson 27. The drifter/reacher would probably sheet through a block at the end of the main boom.

The normal compliment for a storm jib is of course a storm trysail, but fewer and fewer boats carry them any more. For one thing, many craft handle quite well under storm jib alone—this is likely to be true if your boat has a foretriangle equal to the mainsail area or larger, or if your boat does not maneuver well under main alone. In addition, boats equipped with roller reefing can usually reduce the mainsail area enough to simulate the storm trysail in size and shape.

If you do have a trysail, you will probably have to consider a separate track alongside the normal mainsail track, or a system of ties (usually parrel bands) around the mast itself.

Far more sailors complain of too little wind in the sailing season than too much. As a consequence, your natural inclination is likely to be toward a drifter, instead of a storm jib. A drifter, which may be of spinnaker cloth, is normally designed for winds up to 5-7 knots, and more often than not, its shape is spoiled by skippers who can't bear to take it down soon enough. A proper drifter should have leech and foot lines to produce the maximum fullness in the kind of very light airs in which this sail is used. Often a drifter will have no luff snaps at all, or have them fixed at much greater intervals than on normal jibs.

For boats with very large #1 genoas and working jibs, a good intermediate sail is the #2 genoa, cut slightly shorter on the luff and foot and perhaps made of cloth one weight heavier than the #1. A #3 genoa, if carried, is shorter still and is little different, if at all, from the lapper. The number system of describing genoa jibs is so variable as to be almost useless unless one is acquainted with each of the sails on a given boat. The #1 is always the largest genoa and usually the lightest (not counting special sails such as the drifter—also known as a ghoster). The #2 is usually smaller, but is sometimes only heavier. And there are special lightweight #1 genoas—the same size as the standard number one, but of lighter fabric. Some sailors even reverse the number order when talking about standard (non-genoa) jibs: #3 is the largest, and #1 the smallest. It never hurts to ask.

The racer will want at this point to invest in a reaching spinnaker—commonly referred to as a star-cut, from the way the cloths are arranged—and a spinnaker staysail, and possibly one of the new lightweight headsails designed to set alongside the spinnaker on a run. The name of this last sail depends largely on who makes it—chuter, blooper, whatever. There is, alas, no final limit to what can be carried in the way of sails. But unless you're wealthy beyond the dreams of the IRS, or a person to whom winning races is everything, it is seldom wise to buy more than one new sail a season, and even less wise to buy a new fad sail until it has had at least a year to shake itself out.

You may, in fact, sail with great pleasure for years and years under just a main and medium genoa, with a small jib for emergencies. If you have the strength of will to resist the spectacle of a boat the size of yours booming past with her multicolored chute pulling like a team of horses, then you deserve either envy or pity, and I'm not at all sure which.

More sails mean, inevitably, more hardware to handle them. This is something that people frequently forget when ordering a new sail—the cloth may be only part of the tab. It is most demonstrably true in the case of spinnakers. Whatever the sail itself costs, you will also be in for:

Spinnaker halyard, with masthead block, cleat, and possibly winch;
Spinnaker sheets, with turning blocks and padeyes;
Spinnaker pole, with pole lift, downhaul, track, and associated fittings;
Spinnaker sheet winches (maybe).

Anyway, you see what I mean. This gear can run you anywhere from $150 to $500 or more—not counting the winches, not counting installation, and not counting such other goodies as reaching struts, spinnaker nets, or spinnaker turtles.

Assuming the four essential sails—lapper, main, genoa, spinnaker—what sail handling equipment do you really need? In a boat anywhere from 20 to 30 feet, I'd say you will be able to cope if you have the following:

Jib halyard winch,
Main halyard winch (if the main doesn't have a downhaul tackle),
Pair of cockpit sheet winches,
Genoa track with one car port and starboard,
Spinnaker gear as listed above (the short list, that is),
Pair of jib sheet blocks,

(As for sizes, see the equipment lists at the end of this book).

It is, in my opinion, a good idea to buy equipment in advance where possible. If, for instance, you are buying jib sheets, get them long enough so they will serve as genoa sheets when you get around to buying that sail; and buy jib sheet blocks husky enough to stand the extra pull of a jennie even if you don't have one. If you have to make a choice, I think it's far better to have one good set of gear and swap it around than to have two batches of mediocre equipment.

45

Part II. Sailing Principles Amplified

7. Understanding Wind

Wind, as most people know, is merely air in motion, that motion being caused by temperature and pressure differences from place to place. Although the same natural forces are behind major wind systems and local gusts and eddies, the latter are of more immediate concern to the skipper. It helps to know that a cold front is coming, but there's not a great deal one can do about it. Knowledge of local air currents, based on prevailing wind patterns, can be far more useful, both to the cruising or casual sailor and the racer.

Typically, though, it is racing which has produced the most elaborate studies of wind and sailboats, and in order to take full advantage of what the wind does, it's necessary to sail your boat with something approaching the kind of concentration a racer takes for granted.

A couple of basic facts about wind and sails may be enlightening. First, the wind pressure on a surface varies approximately as the *square* of its strength. So a 10-knot breeze is not twice as strong as a 5-knot one, at least not in the effect it has on your boat. It exerts about four times the pressure on your sails, which is one reason why small boats respond so dramatically to puffs and gusts.

Second, determining the true wind strength in which your boat has to function is not as easy as you might think. In his excellent book, *Wind and Sailing Boats* (Quadrangle), Alan Watts examines more closely the question of actual wind speed. (We're talking here about true wind speed, not apparent wind —that comes later.) There is a difference between wind speeds over land and over water. According to Mr. Watts, the mean wind speed over land is roughly half what it is over open water, thanks largely to the friction offered by the ground surface. This finding is reflected not only in the considerably larger number of high wind reports from ships than from land stations, but it has also been noticed—perhaps subconsciously—by anyone who has sailed extensively. While the wind indicators ashore, fluttering leaves and the like, indicate a gentle breeze, the experienced sailor finds himself adding a few knots to that observed strength when calculating what it will be like on the water a mile or so away.

Wind gusts are generally one and a half or two times as strong as the mean wind force ashore. Over water, the gust speed is relatively less, compared to the mean wind speed, but only because the mean wind is so much more forceful. Alan Watts gives a useful rule of thumb for estimating the effective strength of the sailing wind: an average of the mean speed and the gusts. Wind forecast of 10 knots, gusting to 20, suggests then that you should be rigged to take advantage of 15-knot winds.

Of course the boat must also endure the higher gusts and bash through them somehow, while sailing the average wind strength. If there is a great variance between the average strength and the gusts, then I would be inclined to err on the side of too little sail, unless one is sailing an easily righted small craft in enclosed waters.

People who get their weather information secondhand—from the radio or TV—and who seldom check it against reality have a distorted picture of the wind. Although a breeze may blow from one approximate direction at more or less the same strength for days or even weeks without obvious variation, in fact it is changing all the time, both in strength and direction. On a long haul, it's easy to ignore these small changes (especially when sailing off the wind), and the distance lost doesn't amount to much. Besides, it's probably better on a cruise to arrive a half hour later than to irritate the crew continually by having them readjust the sheets or change sails.

But there are times aboard even the most relaxed vessels when one wants or needs to sail the boat at its very best, and to do that you have to be able to judge wind speed and direction accurately.

There is first the question of true and apparent wind, both as to force and direction. Because this distinction is so hard for most people to absorb, it is probably worth the time involved to go over it again. True wind is, of course, what is noted by an observer who is not in motion—at a shore station, or on a boat made fast to a pier. It is the force and direction of the meteorological wind at a given moment.

Apparent wind is the wind one feels when one is moving. It is just as "real" as true wind, in the sense that instruments aboard a moving boat will register apparent, not true, wind force and direction. The apparent wind is a combination of the true wind (if any) and the false wind caused by the vehicle's moving through the air.

Take a real example. Your boat is becalmed in a tide race at slack water. The sails hang limp and the boat is motionless, both relative to the water and to the shore. The current turns and begins to flow, carrying your boat with it. Ashore, flags hang lifeless, smoke rises vertically, but you feel a wind. Your boat rides past an anchored vessel, and her flag is hanging, but your sails fill to a wind apparently coming right against the current. Apparent wind, with a force equal to the speed at which the current is carrying your boat through the still air. In this case, the false wind of motion and the apparent wind are the same.

Later on, out of the current, a 10-knot breeze springs up from astern. You hoist your spinnaker and take off, running dead before the wind. It seems to drop away, and although a boat beating toward you is heeled dramatically, you feel very little breeze. Your boat's speedometer is reading 4 knots, and if you had an anemometer, it would probably indicate that the wind from astern is 6 knots. In this second case, the false wind of 4 knots is directly opposite the true wind, and by subtracting the one from the other, you're left with an apparent wind of 6.

Mostly, though, the situation is not so clearcut as this. You're riding at anchor, and the boat's bow is facing right into a 10-knot west wind. Making sail, you hoist the anchor and beat off to windward. You know that your boat will sail to within 45° of the true wind—other owners have told you so dozens of times. And indeed, as you head off on starboard tack at about 5 knots, the compass reads right around 225°. But the telltale at the masthead shows the wind coming from, at most, 30° off the bow, and the anemometer is now reading 12 or 13 knots. What's happened?

The vector diagram shows exactly: The wind has increased in apparent speed because you're heading more or less into it, creating your false wind of motion to the extent of 5 knots. Since you're not heading directly into the true wind, your 5 knot false wind isn't simply added to the true wind, but a large fraction of it does go to increase the speed of the wind you feel. Likewise, the false wind's direction—right over the bow—tends to pull the apparent wind direction to a point between the false wind and the true wind.

48

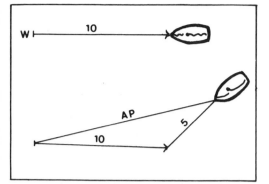

Vector diagram shows what happens when boat anchored in 10-knot wind (top) sets sail close hauled on starboard tack. Boat speed is five knots, and apparent wind (AP) is 12-13 knots.

Thus, when you're reaching beam-on to the true wind, your apparent wind will be coming from forward of the beam at a speed somewhat greater than the true wind. An apparent wind on the beam reflects a true wind coming from over the quarter, and the difference between true and apparent wind direction is proportional to the speed your boat is making (and the false wind of motion it is creating). Obviously, as the boat gains speed—increasing the force of the false wind—the apparent wind's direction will move forward and its speed will increase.

The concept, once learned, is not terribly vital except when you're sailing close-hauled. Then you're likely to make mistakes when trying to guess the course you'll be able to sail on the opposite tack. This is why many sailors' compasses have additional vanes at 45° to the lubber line, to make easier the calculation of where the true wind lies, and what your course on the opposite tack must be.

For trimming sails, however, the only wind that matters is the apparent wind; it's the one which the sails respond to. There are numerous complicated gadgets for registering apparent wind, but for most sailors the simpler wind vanes will do well enough, once one has learned to appreciate the strength of the wind

in terms of what it's doing to the boat.

Ideally the skipper should be able to see from the helm a wind vane operating in clear air on every heading. The only one that qualifies is the masthead fly, and it has drawbacks of its own. To begin with, on many modern boats the masthead is a very crowded place, and it may be difficult to emplace a wind vane among the clutter of burgees, VHF radio antennas, masthead lights and the like. More important, constant gazing at the top of a high aspect ratio mast is almost sure to give the helmsman a savage crick in the neck. And finally, the wind at the masthead is often different, both in force and direction, from the wind down near water level. This last factor is one that applies mostly to larger boats in the cruising sizes, but any spar of 30 feet or so can be operating in considerably different air at the top and bottom.

Consider the points of sailing. Running, you will want a vane that registers clean air coming over the transom and the quarters, and a length of yarn on the backstay will probably survive reasonably well. On a reach, the best place for a telltale is on the windward upper shroud—just where a genoa jib is likeliest to wipe it off when tacking. There is no real solution to the problem, alas. The closest one can come to it is to have a large ball of dark-colored yarn aboard, to replace the shroud telltales as they go.

Beating, when an accurate telltale is most important, is also the most difficult point for placing one. The windward upper shroud is a reasonably good spot, but it can be hard visually to translate the angle of the wool thread into the angle of wind on the sail. Aerodynamically, a vane forward of the forestay—mounted on the pulpit, say—is excellent, but its life is apt to be short. The best solution seems to be light strips on either side of the jib luff, back far enough to escape turbulence from the stay—6 to 12 inches or so. They don't really show the apparent wind

Luff woolies can be strung through a jib or, as here, the forestaysail of a cutter.

relative to the boat, but something rather more important, the wind flow on both sides of the jib. We'll discuss using these telltales in the next chapter.

Estimating wind force comes with time and experience, unless you decide to skip these two and go direct to machinery. Although a devoted gadgeteer, I have a firm mistrust of all the dials I love so much. If you can judge the wind strength without instruments, you'll never have to worry about their breaking down. Perhaps the most important thing to avoid is the futile effort to gauge wind with millimetric precision. Admiral Beaufort of the 19th century Royal Navy was well aware of this (having no suitable instruments of this type anyway). His system of measurement was based on observable effects of the wind on the sea and on shipping. The forces into which the Beaufort Scale is divided are offhand graduations of true wind strengths, keyed to brief phrases and slightly longer descriptions.

The admiral's original table, expressed in terms of the warships of his own day, is not terribly helpful to the pleasure boatman of nearly two centuries later. Various people have attempted to redo the Beaufort Scale in modern language, for both land and sea, with varying success. The difficulty is in adopting terms sufficiently broad to have the same meaning for everyone. Even the sea descriptions can be variously interpreted (height above water, for instance, will have a lot to do with whether one perceives foam or spindrift).

Still the speed categories, especially in the lower ranges and up to about Force 9, have proven useful to many generations of sailors. It is only beyond the point of *Strong gale* that gradations become hard for the amateur. And by that time, if he is still at sea, he's probably better off not knowing. If he survives, he's entitled to any lie he cares to invent.

What I'm suggesting is that the reader who finds the idea of a Beaufort Scale useful would be best advised to create his own. He will probably do no better than the admiral when it comes to wind speed categories or sea descriptions, as reproduced here. When it comes to *Effects Ashore*, the reader should bear in mind Watts' findings about relative speeds of wind on land and sea. Using the Beaufort Scale when ashore to predict what the wind at sea will be like requires a good deal of caution.

Two personal developments of the Beaufort Scale are shown here. One is the work of Thomas Colvin, the well-known designer, cruising authority, and general iconoclast. He is talking about a beefy cruising boat of larger than average size and old-fashioned rig—a point I make only to qualify his sail descriptions. The other is for day-sailers, and was prepared by Ian Proctor, the well-known British designer, mast-maker and sailor. The differences between them will perhaps suggest why anyone who wants to go this route will have to figure out his own guidelines.

BEAUFORT SCALE ADAPTED FOR DINGHY SAILORS

Beaufort Number	General Description	Dinghy Criterion	Velocity in Knots
0	Calm		Less than 1
1	Light air	Helmsman and crew sit on opposite sides of boat to windward.	1 to 3
2	Light breeze	Helmsman and crew sit on the windward side of the boat.	4 to 6
3	Gentle breeze	Helmsman and crew sit out on weather gunwale. Osprey, Hornet, Int. 14, and Merlin-Rockets may plane.	7 to 10
4	Moderate breeze	Helmsman and crew lie out hard over weather gunwale. Nat. 12 and Firefly may plane.	11 to 16
5	Fresh breeze	All racing dinghies have to ease sheets in heavier gusts when beating. Int. 14 reefs.	17 to 21
6	Strong breeze	Int. 14 dinghy reefs to bottom batten.	22 to 27
7	Near gale	Int. 14 reefed to hounds with 6 small jib.	28 to 33
8	Gale	Int. 14 stows jib. Difficult to sail dinghy at all. Nat. 12 under jib only.	34 to 40

Adapted from *Wind and Sailing Boats,* by Alan Watts, Quadrangle Books, Chicago 60611, 1970. Copyright © 1965 by Alan Watts.

The Beaufort Wind Scale, Based on a 36′ Waterline Cruising Vessel

Beaufort Number	Description of Sea	State of Sea	Close Hauled	Broad Reach	Velocity In Knots	Force In LBS/Sq Ft
0	Calm	Smooth, mirror-like.	All sail; 0-1 knot.	All sail; 0-1.5 knots.	0-2.6	.03
1	Light Air	Smooth, small wavelets.	All sail; 1-2 knots.	All sail; 2-3.5 knots.	6.9	.23
2	Light Breeze	Small waves, crests breaking	All sail; vessel heels moderately. 3-4 knots.	All sail; 4-6 knots.	11.3	.62
3	Gentle Breeze	Foam has glossy appearance; not yet white.	Working sail and topsails. 5-6 knots.	Working sails; topsails & light sails; 6-7 knots.	15.6	1.20
4	Moderate Breeze	Larger waves, many "white horses."	Working sail only; Lt Displacement vessels reef. 6-7 knots.	Full working sail & topsails; Lt Displ. hand topsails; 7-8 knots.	20	1.90
5	Stiff Breeze	Waves pronounced; long white foam crests.	All vessels reef; Lt Displacement double reef; 5-6 knots.	Working sails only; 8-9 knots.	24.3	2.90
6	Fresh Breeze	Large waves, white foam crests all over.	Deep reefs; 3-4 knots.	Hvy Displ, small reefs; Lt Displ, deep reefs. 8-9 knots.	29.5	4.20
7	Very Fresh Breeze	Sea heaps up; wind blows foam in streaks.	Hvy Displ, deep reefs; Lt Dis, min. working sail. 2-3 knots.	Deep reefs in largest sail; 8-9 knots.	34.7	5.9
9	Strong Gale	Foam blown in dense streaks.	Lying ahull; sea anchor or drogue out; side drift.	Run off—under bare poles and warps. 3-5 knots.	48.1	11.50
10	Very Strong Gale	High waves; long overhanging crests; Lg. foam patches.	Lying ahull; sea anchor or drogue.	Run off—bare poles & warps; 3-5 knots; speed too great; danger of broaching.	56.4	15.5
11	Violent Gale	High waves	Lie to sea anchor.	Bare poles; sea anchor, warps, drogue; vessel must be slowed down.	65.1	20.6
12	Hurricane; Typhoon	Streaking foam; Spray in air.	Lie to sea anchor.	Lie to sea anchor.	78.1	29.6

from *Coastwise and Offshore Cruising Wrinkles,* by Thomas E. Colvin, copyright © 1972 by Seven Seas Press, New York, N.Y. 10003. Reprinted by permission.

In so doing, it may be useful to begin at Force 4, 11-16 knots, which is often considered the ideal sailing wind for pleasure craft of most sizes. A planing breeze for small boats and a full-sail wind for cruisers, Force 4 makes a good starting point from which to work both ways in developing a personal Beaufort Scale.

One psychological problem with using a Beaufort Scale or anything like it is the tendency to assess a wind at—say—Force 4 and then forget it, until some radical change brings the wind speed again to your attention. In reality, as noted above, the wind speed and direction change constantly, from one moment to the next. The changes can be ignored without disastrous effect, except that in certain situations, notably going to windward, you will sacrifice a lot of efficiency by simply setting the sails and aiming the boat along a compass course.

The farther inshore you sail, the more likely it is that your boat will be affected by gusts, lulls, lifts and headers. (For those who somehow haven't encountered the last two terms, a *lift* is a change in the wind direction which allows you to sail a higher course than before. Conversely, a *header* is a wind shift that forces you to head off to keep the boat's sails full.)

Many of these changes are caused by the interaction of land and water—the shape of the land just behind the shore can funnel or deflect winds, and the composition of the land can create thermal air currents that produce a breeze when everything else is flat calm.

Funneled winds are fairly obvious. One of the most striking and consistent examples in my own experience is sailing down New York's East River when a westerly is blowing across Manhattan Island. This wind is channeled directly down the east-west streets and comes out on the river as a regular series of puffs. Certain of the east-west streets are four lanes instead of the normal two, and the gusts at the wider streets can be strong enough to lay a good size cruiser on her ear.

A more usual funnel effect is at the mouth of a river with high banks or hills on either side, a case frequently encountered at New England harbor entrances. Although the wind may have been blowing at an oblique angle to the shore, the breeze is almost always directly up or down a harbor. And if the wind is opposing the current, a very unpleasant chop can develop in a matter of minutes, which is why it is usually a good idea to plan to enter harbor with wind and current behind you (ideally) or

Funneling effects of trees, houses and the shore. Close to, these obstacles not only divert the wind, but may increase its local strength or blanket it completely.

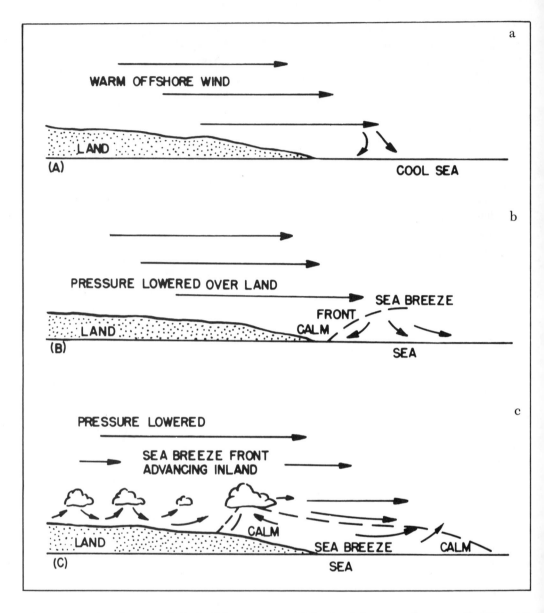

a

WARM OFFSHORE WIND

LAND

(A)

COOL SEA

b

PRESSURE LOWERED OVER LAND

LAND

(B)

SEA BREEZE

FRONT

CALM

SEA

c

PRESSURE LOWERED

SEA BREEZE FRONT
ADVANCING INLAND

LAND

CALM

(C)

SEA BREEZE

CALM

SEA

The sun on a hot day may help build up a sea breeze that overcomes an existing wind off the shore, as shown here: (A) In mid-morning the warm breeze off the land sinks over cool water and begins (B) about noon to create a visible sea breeze, with a calm belt along shore; by mid-afternoon (C) the sea breeze is well established and can be felt well inland, while the calm area has moved offshore.

with both of them on the nose, but not with wind and current against each other.

Even a light breeze off the land will normally continue some distance out over the water. It's a matter of judgment where the most favorable place for sailing will lie, and you have to avoid being blanketed by shoreline structures and at the same time must not sail so far out that the breeze is dissipated. When the wind from the shore is strong, a smaller boat can sail at that distance from shore where the strength is most suitable. Head closer in to avoid the gusts, and diverge from the beach a bit if the wind seems to be slackening. Two important points: Don't neglect the chart in any kind of beach-crawling—you may run out of water or into obstructions while concentrating on moving the boat. And watch out for shorelines that feature high, steep bluffs or cliff formations. Instead of calm in close, there may well be abrupt and unpredictable gusts along the beach, where the winds come right down over the hills.

Sailors have worked with the land and sea breeze for centuries, and in parts of the world sailing commerce depended on these effects for predictable arrivals and departures. Briefly, the land and sea breezes are local winds, produced by the different rates of heating of the shore and the water. Since warm air rises, the air over a heated surface, be it land or water, will tend to rise and other air will move in to replace it. The motion of the replacing air is our thermal breeze.

In most temperate areas, the land begins heating up about midmorning on a sunny day. By early afternoon the ground is relatively hot, and the air above it begins to rise. Cooler air from the water just offshore moves in to replace the heated air, causing a light but definitely useful onshore breeze—called the sea breeze, from its place of origin. How far offshore this breeze will be felt depends, of course, on both the relative temperatures of land and water, and the tendency of the existing wind. It may be that the normal wind and the sea breeze will oppose and cancel each other out. The calm area thus created will normally occur in a fairly narrow band, with onshore breeze on one side of the calm and the existing offshore breeze on the other. On the other hand, the prevailing wind and the thermal sea breeze may reinforce each other.

The sea breeze may get up to 10 knots or so and will normally endure until the evening cools off the land. As night falls, the land loses its heat far faster than the water, until the sea is warmer, and the breeze reverses itself, blowing off the land. The nighttime land breeze, which may last until dawn, is usually much lighter than the sea breeze, and may not come in at all. It is obviously a tricky wind to depend upon, since you must sail fairly close to a dimly perceived shore to use it.

Both land and sea breeze normally blow at right angles to the shore. In fact, the wind generally will change its direction alongshore (as will waves) to blow more directly across the shoreline than its direction offshore might have suggested.

Most people are aware that wind causes waves. Specifically, four things determine wave size and direction: the speed of the wind, the direction from which it is blowing, the duration of the wind, and the distance over which it has blown. Sizable waves can be formed only when the wind has been blowing hard for some time over an extended distance of water. The tables which follow show how this information is codified.

(A) Maximum wave height, unlimited fetch, related to steady wind speed:

Wind Speed [Knots]	Wave Height [Feet]	Wind Speed [Knots]	Wave Height [Feet]
8	3	35	30
12	5	39	36
16	8	43	39
19	12	47	45
27	20	51	51
31	25		

(B) Increase in wave height related to fetch, at steady wind speed:

Wind Speed [Knots]	Fetch in Nautical Miles					
	10	50	100	300	500	1,000
10	2	2	2	2	2	2
15	3	4	5	5	5	5
20	4	7	8	9	9	9
30	6	13	16	18	19	20
40	8	18	23	30	33	34
50	10	22	30	44	47	51

(C) Wave height related to wind speed and duration, but not fetch:

Wind Speed [Knots]	Duration of Wind [Hours]						
	5	10	15	20	30	40	50
10	2	2	2	2	2	2	2
15	4	4	5	5	5	5	5
20	5	7	8	8	9	9	9
30	9	13	16	17	18	19	19
40	14	21	25	28	31	33	33
50	19	29	36	40	45	48	50
60	24	37	47	54	62	67	69

(Wave heights in feet)

On occasion, a wind shift will produce for a short time a confused sea in which some waves, still responding to the former wind, are moving from one direction, while new waves are coming from a considerably different point, creating a sort of herringbone pattern on the sea which can be very difficult to steer into. Too, a distant storm may push out swells that travel a great distance and appear as a separate formation underlying the local wave system.

While waves more or less follow the direction of the wind, it is well to remember that the wind's constant shifting back and forth means that a wave system will seldom exactly coincide with the wind direction for long. Steering the boat—except, of course, when the waves get to be of a dangerous steepness—should be done according to the wind, not the seas.

8. Improving Performance Windward Sailing

Moving your boat to windward effectively is one of the more satisfying sensations in sailing. Cruising sailors habitually sneer at racers' concentration on windward performance at the expense of ease and comfort, but that attitude (I feel) partly reflects most cruising skippers' inability to get their boats to move well to weather at all. Sour grapes.

To be sure, it does require both concentration and forethought to get the most out of a boat on any heading, but there's a lot of ground between the man who is too lazy to do anything about tacking through 100° when it could be 90°, and the skipper who has his whole crew lining the windward rail, except for sail trimming every 15 seconds or so. In this chapter I'd like to suggest some ways to improve your windward performance; how much effort you care to expend is up to you.

But before you can improve any performance, you've got to have a way of assessing it and a yardstick to measure against. A speedometer, even if inaccurate in its measure of miles per hour (and most of them are), will still reflect changes in relative speed

responding to sail adjustment. Even better, if yours is a stock boat popular locally, arrange with another skipper in your class to take turns sailing head to head. Begin as near as possible with the same tuning, the same sails, trimmed the same way. Then use one boat as the control while the other tests various adjustments to see if they increase or reduce speed.

Above all, take the trouble to record what you did and how it worked. The more your sailing records build up, the better answers you'll be able to produce for new situations. By the end of your first season with a new boat, you should have a good idea of what sail combination to set in response to each major wind change. If you try sail changes when you're not racing or trying to get to harbor before dark, you'll have time to experiment more fully, and your results will be more valid.

Even beginning sailors know the basic rules involved in sailing to windward. In a small boat, the weights should be more or less forward—far enough toward the bow to keep the boat level, not so far that the boat begins to dive. The flatter the boat's bottom, the flatter she should be sailed, and seldom at more than 20° of heel in any case. Beyond that, many sailors feel that if one carries maximum sail and straps it in tight, the rest is helmsmanship.

Not if you take your windward sailing seriously, it isn't. Aboard today's ocean racers, it is usual to sail with all sheets uncleated, in a constant process of adjustment to get the most advantageous relationship of sail to wind and sail to sail. Let's begin with the jib, since that's the sail which does the most work getting the modern sloop to windward.

Each of your jibs should have a set of telltales threaded through the sailcloth at three approximately equidistant points up the

This Ericson 29 is going well with the aid of a deck-sweeping genoa having four pairs of luff woolies. Note the small window behind the key wooly, about a third the way up. With this kind of sail, either a window or a lookout to leeward is vital.

luff. The telltales—knitting yarn will do well—should be no more than 6 inches long and anywhere from 6 to 12 inches in from the sail luff. The exact distance will depend on the size of the jib, and you can tape a telltale in place and check it before pushing the yarn through with a darning needle. The yarn itself should be dark enough so it shows through the sail: Under most conditions, you should be able to see both streamers.

In many cases, skippers will put at least one window in the sail at a point where the leeward streamer will show. A window in the average decksweeping genoa isn't a bad thing anyway: When beating, a 150% genoa will block off about a quarter of the helmsman's horizon. The idea is that when the matching tufts of wool on opposite sides of a sail are streaming aft, the airflow over both sides of the jib is smooth and nonturbulent. If the windward tuft begins to lift and then twirl, it means you're sailing too close to the wind, whose flow has separated from the sail. Likewise, when the leeward streamer flutters and spins, it means that you're headed too far off the wind. Either sail higher or ease sheets.

Some very fierce sailors equip their jibs with a horizontal line of streamers, each fastened at the forward edge and each about three inches long. The foremost streamer is just in from the luff, at a spot equally distant from sail snaps up and down the luff. According to Southern California sailor Arvel Gentry, who invented the system, it should be possible to sail with the whole line of tufts streaming aft, or at least with only the foremost one lifting slightly.

Accurate and delicate as the arrangement of "Gentry tufts" may be, the one closest to the luff wire will probably spend a good deal of its time tangled.

Having determined at the mooring or pier which jib to set, you sail out to open water and make sail. In all but the very lightest conditions, the first thing you want from your headsail is a taut, straight luff. Scallops in the luff are the mark of the amateur or the sailor who doesn't care. If your halyards are rope, you may have to take up on them after a bit of sailing, when the stretch in the halyard makes itself felt along the luff. Because of the great friction of luff snaps on the forestay, it takes time for the stress at the masthead and the looseness at the jib tack to even out. For this reason, somesailboats are equipped with downhauls at the tack—either a tackle or a line led back through a block to a spare winch.

In any case, start with a taut luff. The jib may have vertical wrinkles along the luff before the sail has filled with wind, but these should disappear once the jib begins to draw. If they don't, the sail is up too hard. Horizontal wrinkles, on the other hand, mean the luff is too slack.

Adjustments to the jib can be made in several ways, at all three corners: The jib luff is tightened or loosened as required by the halyard and (if the boat is so equipped) the downhaul or Cunningham. This latter piece of gear is similar to the Cunningham on the mainsail. It consists basically of a grommet

sewn into the jib luff with a line run from the tack fitting up through the grommet and then back down to a block at the tack. Strain on the line tautens the luff, and if the jib has a stretchy luff, the Cunningham can be used to lengthen the hoist slightly.

The halyard and downhaul adjust the sail's shape. In most jibs, the point of maximum draft (or fullness) is between 35 and 45% aft of the luff, and under no circumstances more than 50% back. At a given halyard tension, the draft moves aft when the wind blows harder, so that when one sails in a strong wind, it's good tactics to set the halyard up extra hard.

For most purposes, however, once the sail is up, the major adjustments are made with

This sheet lead on a Vega 27 is suitable for a big lapper or small genoa. For a longer-footed sail, the sheet lead block would go back near the aft end of the track and the sheet would probably have to be led back through the turning block attached to the pushpit, then forward to the winch in order to obtain a fair lead.

the jib sheet. The first item of trim is the placement of the jib sheet leads. Most boats have a track running along the gunwale from just aft of the shrouds all the way back (in many cases) to the transom. Depending on the jib being used, the lead blocks can be set anywhere along this track, although in practice the sheet leads are normally established for a given sail and left that way.

Sailing to windward, it was normal practice in earlier years to set the jib lead so the sheet ran at an angle slightly lower than the miter line of the sail. Recently the trend has been to establish an initial lead that runs quite sharply down to the deck. The angle bisected by the jib sheet has no significance in itself; the point is that when the sail luffs, it should luff evenly from head to foot. And while sailing, there should be equal tension on the jib leech and clew.

If you employ a downhaul on your jib, and use it while under way, you may have to change the placement of the jib sheet leads because you've raised or lowered the clew of the sail and changed the angle at which the sheet comes into its block.

The closer the jib sheet is trimmed, the higher the boat can sail—up to the point where the slot between main and jib narrows so much that the air cannot pass efficiently.

This slot should have essentially parallel walls, formed by the jib leech and the leeward belly of the main. To get the best idea of what the slot really looks like, try sighting through it from someone else's boat. Failing that, look aft and up from a point on deck toward the bow.

As boat speed drops, a fuller sail works better, with the fullness fairly low in the sail.

On most boats in the racing fleet, an additional adjustment device called a *Barber hauler* is now standard equipment. Invented by two San Diego brothers named Barber for use on their Lightning, the Barber hauler takes many forms, but does the same thing. It

Jib-mainsail slot on a San Juan 26 close reaching in a light breeze.

The wide angle lens exaggerates this jib-mainsail slot broad reaching, but the essential relationship can still be seen.

provides for a thwartships change in sheet lead, so the sheet angle moves amidships in lulls and outboard in puffs by 8 to 12°, closing or opening the slot between main and jib.

Like the jib, the main can be trimmed in a number of ways, and although there is the complication of the main boom to keep in mind, the reasons for and methods of trimming the main are similar to those involving the jib. Nearly all racing boats today adjust luff tension on the main with a Cunningham, rigged much like the one described for the jib. This, it seems to me, is inherently less satisfactory than a tack downhaul, except if one has to worry about the technicalities of rating the mainsail area. With a downhaul, one has the additional option of setting the full main a foot or so higher or lower on the mast, whereas with luff adjustment by Cunningham, the sail is always at full height unless it's reefed.

An unusual, cockpit-wide mainsheet traveler aboard a Danish sloop. The after third of each seat is raised to provide better visibility for the person at the helm.

On the wind in heavy air, one takes up on the halyard, the tack downhaul (if any) and the foot outhaul, making the sail flat, with draft well forward. As the wind lightens, one can ease the downhaul or the halyard, and slack off slightly on the outhaul (too much slack along the boom will usually result in nothing but a series of vertical ridges along the foot of the sail).

The traveler, too, plays an important part in maintaining sail shape. Nearly all modern sloops have gone to extended travelers, some running the width of the boat, in order to be able to trim the boom with a straight downward pull even when it is not over the center of the boat. Once beyond the traveler's extent, of course, the boom is trimmed downward by the vang.

Trimming the main boom down reduces the falling-off at the head of the sail which is called *twist*. (The same effect is obtained for the jib by moving the sheet block forward.) Not all twist in a sail is bad, but in general, twist means that the upper part of a sail has a different angle of attack to the wind than does

With a transom cutout like the one on this O'Day 23, a full-width traveler aft is obviously impossible. This is one solution.

One way of having a reasonably wide traveler that isn't in the cockpit or across the transom is to put it on the cabin roof over the main hatch, as on the Northwest 21.

the lower part—which in turn means that the sail as a whole cannot be properly trimmed.

Draft in the main is and should be somewhat further back in the sail than it is in the jib—about halfway, says Steve Colgate, perhaps the best known of today's sailing school proprietors. This results in a somewhat different shape to the main. When working up to windward, it will be necessary to alternate between strapping the main into a flat curve with the draft aft, for pointing high, and then letting the sail become fuller, moving the draft forward, for acceleration.

When sailing to windward in steep seas, it may be necessary to ease the jib and head off. Generally it's better in choppy conditions to keep the boat moving rather than to concentrate on pointing high. Conversely, when you're able to sail in strongish winds and sheltered waters, your boat will probably point her highest. Expert sailors have decided, after much controversy, that it almost always pays to tack when you're headed by a gust, if the pattern of the gusts is such that they seem to be lasting at least a couple of minutes. To help you decide whether tacking is indicated, you should have an accurate idea of your boat's normal time to tack, from the moment when the helm is put over to the point on the opposite tack when full sailing speed is attained.

For complex reasons having to do with the effect of the spinning earth on wind direction, most gusts cause the wind to veer—that is, to change its direction clockwise—in the Northern Hemisphere (and vice versa in the Southern). What this means is that if you're sailing close-hauled, it's better to be on starboard tack in a gust. The wind will normally move aft slightly, freeing the boat. As the gust ends, it may well pay to tack quickly over to port for the lull, to avoid being headed.

The best windward course, then, is not at all a straight line or a series of equal-length zigzags. Working to windward (an accurate as well as expressive phrase) is a continual effort to move the boat to best advantage relative to wind and sea. Of course the smaller boat will be much quicker to tack and much more responsive to wave action, so where a daysailer may tack again and again, a cruising boat's skipper may feel that his vessel would lose more than she could gain by coming about for each small header. A heavy cruising boat is likely to be able to drive right through small gusts with only a momentary luff and no great loss in boat speed, where a light-displacement craft will be stopped dead.

The art of tacking is one that depends almost entirely on two things—rudder action and timing. An actual tack can take from 10 seconds to half a minute or more (count off 30 seconds, and see for yourself just how long *that* is), but more important is the technique of preserving the boat's forward motion through a tack. Slamming the tiller over will bring the bow around fast enough, but it will also stop nearly any boat dead in the water. With the exception of a very few craft that consistently land in irons, it's a bad idea to hold the jib on the old tack long enough to let it back. A backed jib will of course throw the bow around, but it will also stop forward speed almost completely.

Sailing the boat through the turn is far better. Begin with a moderate amount of helm, enough to turn your bow quickly into the wind without pivoting so fast that the rudder drags badly. As the boat turns, more helm can be applied. The crew lets go the jib a split second after it begins to luff and takes in the slack on the other sheet—but no more than the slack. A lot of good tacks are ruined by overeager crews getting the sheet in too fast and backwinding the jib on the new tack.

As the bow comes through the eye of the wind, the tiller should begin to straighten out, and the boat should still be moving ahead. Here's where a good wind vane is worth its weight in diamonds. When the fluttering luff of the jib passes the centerline, the jib hand can start filling the sail. It should be set and drawing as the bow comes around to the new heading relative to the wind. Remember that you invariably lose some forward speed when tacking, which means the apparent wind moves aft. So as you square off on the new tack, the wind will be a little freer than when the boat picks up speed (maintaining the same compass heading), and the apparent wind goes forward.

On a larger boat, the wincher and tailer handling the jib sheet must develop precise teamwork. As the sheet first comes in, it's a hand-over-hand operation, and only as the sail fills will it pay to begin cranking. With really good timing and in a light wind, the winch handle should be used—if at all—only for the last 6 inches or so of sheet. Be ready, as the boat moves off on the new tack, to readjust the sheet as required. Even when the boat is at the same heading relative to the wind on each tack, the seas may cause perceptibly different kinds of sailing. Striking the bows at an angle only a few degrees different from the wind direction, waves can stop a boat in her tracks, especially the larger waves left over in a falling wind.

On small boats, tacking is much more a matter of crew weight shift. With the current spaghetti-factory aspect of modern daysailers, it's vital for skipper and crew to be able to shift from one side of the boat to the other without becoming tangled in line. The actual weight shift is usually best done almost as a rhythmic dance step, as the boat comes about. Sitting on the high side, get your forward leg (left leg on port tack, right leg on starboard) across without transferring your weight. As the bow comes through the wind, you move across the boat, shifting your weight from one foot to the other, your stern facing the boat's bow.

Obviously this maneuver has to be done in a crouch, and it must also be planned and practiced to avoid vangs and sheets. Boom across and steadying on the new tack, the crew is handling the jib at about the same time he is sitting down and getting his second leg across.

In a small boat with a less-than-masthead jib, the main does proportionally more of the work, and there is less jib sheet to haul anyway than when dragging a genoa clear across the boat. Once settled on a new tack, coil the sheets neatly and, if you're anticipating more tacks, set up the windward jib sheet on the winch to save a couple of seconds later. It seldom pays to put less than three turns on a winch, by the way; if you need the thing at all, you'll require at least that much friction.

If, as in many boats, the lead from sheet block to winch is at a sharp angle, causing an abnormal number of sheet wraps (when a turn with stress winds up on top of another), give thought to adding a second block on the sheet track, as far from the winch as you can get it, to provide the flattest possible lead. You may, if the genoa track is too short, have to take the lead all the way back to the quarter.

When engaged simultaneously in a series of tacks and a change of headsails, it is often tempting to lead both sheets on one side of the boat, taking strain on the old jib with one, and setting the other up to the clew of the new jib, ready to go. There is nothing wrong with this, *if* you make sure to get the sheet off the detached jib and led back around the windward side: Never allow your boat to be crippled by being unable to come about or jibe at a moment's notice.

Deciding the most productive moment at which to tack (wind shifts aside) can be difficult. It is nearly always a fight between logic and wishful thinking: Logic tells you that there's no point in coming about until you're at least at right angles to the mark you hope to clear; hope eternal tells you that almost right angles is the same as 90°. It's not.

For navigational purposes, government marks are very handy as tacking points, but do remember that buoys weren't put there for that purpose. Especially when close in to shore, they usually mark shoals or channel edges. Even if your boat is shallow enough to ride over the bar, there may well be an exaggerated current around the buoy, caused by water rushing through a narrowing space, like air in the jib-mainsail slot. This current may help you or make you tack short—just so you have some idea in advance what's going to happen. If you see the current is killing you, tack early and get away.

9. Improving Your Technique Running and Reaching

In this chapter we'll concentrate on running and reaching without the spinnaker, saving the chute for consideration by itself. This in spite of my feeling that any boat equipped to carry a spinnaker ought to have one as part of its essential sail wardrobe.

Without a chute, however, it's still possible to improve a boat's performance downwind at minimum expense. As opposed to windward sailing, running requires a sail plan that offers maximum surface to the wind without being hopelessly overbalanced. On una or cat rigs, and on older boats with small jibs, balance under main alone should be adequate, but the newer sloops, with masts nearly amidships, really require significant and functioning sail area forward.

For one thing, while the boat will move downwind under main alone, it will be badly unbalanced, attempting to luff up at every opportunity. For another, the so-called mainsail of a modern sloop is often far less than the area of the foretriangle, never mind an overlapping jib.

But the mainsail is still there to be used. It should be set and trimmed to offer a large, full

On a broad reach, the vang helps keep the boom from cocking and the sail from twisting, although this main is probably too flat for the light air conditions.

surface at right angles to the wind, since it's been shown that the bulbous shape of a spinnaker is more effective downwind than a flat, wall-like surface of equivalent outside dimensions. This means slacking the luff by easing the downhaul (usually the sail should be as high as it will go, so you don't want to slack the halyard); softening the foot by easing the outhaul and/or unzipping the foot; puckering the leech by taking up a bit on the leech line.

With the main swung out, a vang or preventer is absolutely vital. Even in light airs, an unexpected jibe does not help the cause, and the wake of rather a small powerboat can snap the boom across. A vang also helps cut down on twist—in this case, caused by the boom's tendency to rise as wind fills the sail. Although baggy, the sail should retain as much cross-sectional area as you can manage. Vangs, which these days are often multi-part tackles, are too easy to pull sometimes: A lightweight can drag the boom down with little effort, and he does. *Easy does it* is

the motto for downwind trimming.

Ordinary jibs are a pain going downwind. They often refuse to draw or, worse, fill in a sullen fashion and then expire after five seconds. It's worth the effort to keep them filled, however, especially if they are of any size at all. Directly downwind in mild conditions, a reasonably skilled hand should have no trouble keeping the jib drawing opposite the main. It may be a good idea to move the trim point for the jib sheet to the most outboard position on the track, or even aft to the quarter blocks.

Far better, and an excellent investment in any case, is a telescoping whisker pole. Lighter than a spinnaker pole, the whisker pole used to be standard equipment on every cruising boat and many daysailers. It rigs with a spring jaw to an eye on the mast or deck, and through the clew grommet of the jib at the other end, using either a duplicate jaw or a simple, easily disengaged pin. No topping lift or downhaul should be necessary, and the pole should be capable of winging out the largest jib aboard in a smooth curve.

The jib is then trimmed with the sheet alone, simply and without frills. No one has developed frills for the whisker pole because (I suspect) they've been too busy working over the spinnaker boom.

Trim downwind, as most people remember, requires that movable weights move themselves aft. The less buoyancy a boat carries forward, the more important this weight shift is. And as the wind rises, it can become crucial: a running boat has the tendency to put its nose down and may even drive right under in certain brisk conditions. If you're running and see that you're beginning to take solid water over the bows, it's time to let up and set a smaller jib.

Running in any sort of sea requires first-rate helmsmanship—it is quite different from moving a boat to windward, as the pressures on the tiller will go from quite dead at one moment to back-breaking at the next. The quantity of water turned by the rudder is often sufficient at high speeds to rip off pintles, grudgeons or both, if the boat broaches suddenly.

Remember that when running the boat's forward speed is subtracted from the true wind, so the apparent wind will be significantly stronger once the boat heads up. Consider also that when heading downwind on a choppy day, the whitecaps are far less visible from upwind. If the boat should broach, then, you're likely to find you've gone in an instant from a lively sleighride in a reasonable breeze to a howling gale with spray breaking over the deck. It's probably not as bad as it seems, but the transition can be unsettling.

Under certain circumstances a condition known as "rhythmic rolling" will begin. The name describes it well. The boat begins to roll first to one side, then the other, increasing her maximum angle of heel each time until finally she broaches, capsizes upwind (if a small boat), to trips her boom in the water. The way to break this vicious cycle is simple: just change the boat's heading by a few degrees, and she'll shake herself free.

Without a spinnaker, most boats will only broach to windward if they get out of control while surfing; unless of course you're sailing without a vang on the main, and the boom slams over. If you must sail downwind without a vang, then make sure that the mainsheet is constantly tended in any kind of wind, ready to run with half a turn around a cleat. A good sheet handler can minimize the effects of an unintentional jibe considerably, by keeping the boom off the rigging far enough so that, when a jibe comes, there's room enough to let the sheet run a bit and avoid the sudden, shattering whack of spar against shrouds.

Unfortunately, it's almost impossible to avoid talking about jibes as if the maneuver were inherently vicious. It's not. Properly executed, there is no danger in it. The sailor should fix in his mind that jibing is neither more nor less acceptable as a way of changing direction than is tacking. Reaching is the misunderstood point of sailing, so much so that no one seems really to be certain if it's one point or three. Just how different from each other are close, beam and broad reaching, anyway? I would venture to say that if one has a spinnaker and makes the most of it, all sailing can be redivided into windward sailing and spinnaker sailing. Leaving the chute out of the picture for the moment, reaching is still a valid concept, but only if one considers it as a spectrum of relative directions, not as a differentiated series of arbitrary "points."

Close reaching really amounts to almost-beating. The principle difference between the two is that on a close reach there is the possibility of sheet adjustment both in and out: you have the choice of hardening up if necessary. The main boom is trimmed at or

Reaching off like a train, with the sheet and vang acting together to keep the boom down. Notice the small amount of twist in the mainsail; the jib sheet appears to be fouled on the lifeline stanchion.

close to the end of the traveler, but both jib and main are still flat in shape, for maximum lift.

As the boat turns away from the wind, and the sheets are eased, the boom will tend to rise, and at this point a vang will begin to be helpful. Easing the jib sheet will increase the twist in the head of that sail, and the best way to eliminate it—presuming that you're sailing with a vanged mainsail—is to move the sheet block forward. This increases the pull down the jib leech, decreasing twist. If you don't have a vang, and the boom cannot be kept down, the mainsail will begin to twist. In order to keep the slot's sides more or less parallel, you'll have to accept a certain amount of jib twist too. In fact you may even want to move the jib sheet block aft a bit to ease tension on the leech.

Still further off the wind, broad reaching or beam reaching, you can trim the sails as if for running, except that the jib will of course still be on the same side of the boat as the main. Coming onto a broad reach, with the apparent wind over the quarter, you may have to trim the main in a bit more than you otherwise would, in order to keep the jib pulling well. By this stage, sail controls are nearly in their normal downwind position.

Beam and (in heavy winds) broad reaching are often the fastest points of sailing for any boat, and tend to be the most stimulating in the sense that there's a lot of sense of motion. The noise and spray can, however, take the crews' minds off the continuing necessity for sail trim, and frequently the rush of the boat through the water is more sound than speed. Unless you are very familiar with your boat, continue to trim according to the apparent wind, not the water being thrown about.

Chief villain is usually the sailor's habit of trimming sheets too much when on or near a beam reach. The boat heels somewhat more, and white water races along the lee rail—in actuality, by dragging those chain plates you

may simply be creating more hull friction. The boat may move more easily, if somewhat less dramatically, if you let her up. Here is a particular situation where having a twin sailing alongside can be immeasurably helpful in determining who's going faster, and then in discovering why.

10. Spinnakers and Other Light Sails

Time was, and not so very long ago, that the most immediate difference between racing boats and others was the possession of a spinnaker by the former. Nowadays, of course, a racer with only one spinnaker is (to paraphrase a current ad campaign) like a Boeing 746-1/2, and more and more cruisers are turning to the spinnaker as a very useful and surprisingly docile sail both downwind and reaching. My own feelings about owning a chute have already been aired—it is one of the things that makes a sailboat fun, and if your boat can set one and your bank account handle one, you ought to own a spinnaker.

Before plunging into the setting and trimming of spinnakers, a small refresher in terminology may be handy. Because the spinnaker's effect on a boat's performance can be so dramatic, many skippers feel that if they aren't flying a chute, they're being cheated somehow. They may be right, yet there are chutes and chutes, and proper times to fly each (or none at all).

Spinnakers may be classified according to the point of sailing for which they're designed—running, general reaching and close-reaching (the fashionable star-cut is largely synonymous with the last condition). Bruce Banks, the British sailmaker who invented the star-cut, doesn't like to have spinnakers graded in this fashion, however, because he says it suggests that no one can make a good all-purpose chute. For him, the gradations are *floater, worker* and *star-cut*: The first is for very, very light airs, the second for running and reaching most of the time, the last for close-reaching and for use in heavy weather. Banks is inclined to feel, he says, that if the wind is too strong for a star-cut, then a so-called storm spinnaker probably won't serve either, so why have one?

In shape, a spinnaker—the normal variety, anyway—somewhat resembles two sections of a parachute. There is a center seam running from top to bottom, and horizontal bands of cloth—usually an excuse for the use of color—cut from lightweight nylon. Generally speaking, the flatter the sail is cut, the closer to windward it can be carried.

The star-cut developed because more sailors wanted to carry their spinnaker (by far the largest sail on the boat) closer to the wind. Being secured only at the corners, a chute of light nylon will distort badly as the apparent wind moves forward and becomes stronger. The star-cut's design is based on the fact that the forces in a flying sail radiate out from the three corners, and this sail is therefore of most use in conditions that are worst for conventionally cut spinnakers. It is a flat sail, with radiating cloths from head and clews, and as must be obvious, it is complicated to cut and wastes a good deal of material in the process.

All spinnakers have the same shifting terminology because of their symmetrical shape. There is the head, at the top, usually identifiable even when the sail is a pile of cloth on the floor by being the only corner grommet with a swivel. The two lower corners are called clews and the sides leeches; or they are until the sail is set. Then the edge of the sail held out to windward by the spinnaker pole becomes the sail's luff, the corner at the lower end of the luff is the tack, while the remaining side and corner are still leech and clew, respectively.

The sail is controlled by three lines as well as the pole: The spinnaker halyard is led from a block at the masthead, above and forward of the intersection of mast and highest forestay; the two spinnaker sheets are identical until the sail is hoisted, when the one on the pole side is renamed the guy. If the sail should be jibed (not as horrendous a thought as it seems at first), the names of the sail and lines are swapped side for side: the old sheet is the new guy and vice versa; the tack becomes the clew and the luff the leech. And also vice versa. Only the head and foot remain the same.

Because all three of the spinnaker's sides are free, the controls at the corners and the hardware associated with them are critical. We've already mentioned the spinnaker halyard; this line and the block it runs through are subject to much twisting and jamming, especially when the spinnaker halyard is an

All the spinnaker's controls can be clearly seen in this photo of an Ericson 25. The sheet and guy are not led all the way back to the quarters but to more convenient and just as effective turning blocks on the genoa track. Note the backstay tensioner, multi-part mainsheet and vang: This boat is equipped for serious work.

afterthought installation on older spars, with less than ideal clearance above the forestay. Under normal sailing conditions, when the chute is not in use, many skippers snap the business end of the halyard to the pulpit and cleat the other at the base of the mast. This practice does nothing for windward efficiency, but it does keep the two ends of the halyard separate.

Other skippers double-end the halyard by putting a snap at each end, and run the ends to eyes port and starboard near the shrouds. When you remember that the spinnaker halyard must be led to one side of the forestay or the other, and outside of absolutely every other piece of rigging, this idea seems more acceptable. It does, however, mean that the hand detailed to raise the chute has an extra task to remember, since he must free the pulling end of the halyard before he can use it.

While a spinnaker may set downwind without being extended by a pole (in fact, it will do so during a jibe), the spinnaker boom is necessary most of the time. It's usually a stout aluminum spar with an identical spring-loaded jaw fitting at each end, operable from the center of the pole by lanyards. There is also a sling to support the pole from above, and a similar fitting underneath. The upper side of the pole is normally the one to which the open jaws face; when attached, the jaws look up, so the force of gravity will release them when the holding pin is withdrawn.

The spinnaker sheet and guy should be (like any sheet) heavy enough to do the job without being so heavy they drag the sail down. Spinnaker sheets are normally secured to the clews by snap shackles. The outer jaw of the spinnaker pole may be secured to a ring at the tack of the sail, or the guy may simply be run through the jaw itself: When the sail is trimmed, the pole will normally move as far toward the tack as the splice in the end of the guy will permit.

The inner end of the pole is snapped to a

A normally-cut chute setting beautifully on a beam reach. Without a strut, the guy lead is somewhat improved by running it through a genoa block well forward.

ring on the forward side of the mast. In all but the smallest boats, this ring is mounted on a short, vertical length of track, allowing the pole's inner end to be raised or lowered as the sail trim requires. But the pole is far too heavy to be allowed simply to hang on the corner of the chute. Instead, it has its own halyard——more properly called a *lift*—led upward from the pole sling or from a balance point on the pole to a block on the forward side of the mast well below the spreaders. Under some circumstances the spinnaker will try to fly up with the outer end of the pole, so that's controlled by the pole foreguy, a light line that runs from the bottom of the pole to a block on deck near the bow, then aft to the mast.

In larger boats, when the spinnaker is flown on a reach the trim angle of the guy is impossible, dragging around the shrouds and coming to the pole at an acute angle. An additional pole called the reaching strut is used to keep the guy off the shrouds and, more important, to widen the angle between guy and spinnaker pole, to avoid buckling the pole when winching in the guy in a strong wind. The strut is a short pole with one snap jaw and one open jaw containing a roller, into which the guy fits.

The normal spinnaker sheet and guy lead is well aft in the boat—traditionally right at the quarters. In older boats this worked well—the sheet blocks were out of the way when not in use, and the lead from all the way aft was ideal for the sheet. With flatter chutes, this is sometimes not the case any more, and especially when one is talking about the newer cruisers with fat middles and pinched-in sterns. When you want the widest sheeting position, it's likely to be considerably forward.

Spinnaker sheets are thus generally run through snatch blocks, pieces of hardware that ought at least to double as imperial earrings, which they strongly resemble in price. A snatch block is one which opens at the side, one cheek being hinged and the other latched. Most snatch blocks are also fitted with snap shackles for quick change of location. Personally, I have got along without them for two boats now with minimal loss of efficiency. It can be done if you plan ahead.

Finally there is the question of spinnaker sheet winches. Since a spinnaker, to be effective, must be trimmed constantly, and since the trimmer really has to be able to see the sail, the ideal place for a spinnaker sheet winch is forward in the cockpit, where the trimmer can see under the mainsail. Too, it's more and more common to carry other headsails along with spinnakers—even the genoa, sometimes—and this necessitates a winch for the jib sheet. Or maybe it does—only your banker knows for sure.

In a boat of any size, it takes a crew of three to handle a chute properly, though it can be done with fewer. In the moments when the sail is being raised—which is when the majority of spinnaker screw-ups occur—four people are even better. Once the sail is up, two can cope with the boat—although, again, three is safer, and essential on larger cruisers or in a brisk wind.

When raising or lowering a main or jib, at least one edge of it is fully under control. Not so with the spinnaker. It can spin or wind itself into a tight knot (usually embracing the forestay) if not prepared for hoisting with some care. In sailors' descriptive language, this kind of wrap is often called hourglassing, because the upper and lower halves of the chute remain filled with wind, while the twisted middle contracts more and more tightly around the wire.

One standard precaution taken by most skippers is the setting or permanent rigging of

The simplest kind of spinnaker net, formed by three pieces of shock cord attached to sliding fittings on the forestay.

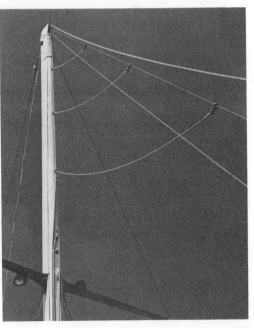

a spinnaker net. This can be an elaborate skeleton of a jib snapped to the forestay and trimmed back to fill the foretriangle; more practical for most people is a permanent installation consisting of one, two, or three lengths of fabric-covered rubber shock cord. Each length runs in a lazy curve from an eye in the forward side of the mast to a ring which runs up and down the forestay. The shock

Hoisting the chute from its sailbag aboard a Hirondelle catamaran. Without a spinnaker turtle, one crewmember will probably have to help the sail from the bag. Even though there is plenty of room on the deck of this little cat, the halyard man's weight would be better aft. Since a spinnaker, unlike a main, should be hoisted fast, it just has to be all squared away in advance. Once up, the sail is trimmed—for a reach in this case, with the pole just off the forestay.

cord is resilient enough to keep the chute from creeping around the stay, but it can be pushed up the stay by the top snap of a masthead jib.

Obviously a certain amount of calculation is required to figure out how much cord beyond a straight-line length is required for each fitting. Plotting the distance from mast to stay on a drawing of the sail plan, and then swinging the line upward, will show you how much stretch you need. Probably you don't want to stretch the shock cord more than a third of its length again if it's to last a whole season out in the open.

There are several approaches to preparing a spinnaker for hoisting. Aboard small boats a tube is frequently recessed into the foredeck. The spinnaker is drawn into the tube by a lanyard sewn to a reinforcing patch in the center of the sail, and led back under the deck to the cockpit. When the sail is fully retracted,

only its corners are accessible, and it can be hoisted quickly and easily.

Mostly, however, the spinnaker installation is temporary—even momentary. You can hoist the chute out of its bag, out of a specialized bag called a turtle, or right from the deck, after restraining the sail with a series of light, string bindings called stops.

One thing which is emphatically *not* recommended is trying to fly a chute from a pile lying on the deck, as it can easily escape over the side to form (if halyard and sheets are made fast) a giant sea anchor.

The best place to ready a spinnaker for hoisting is ashore, on a large, clean floor or a healthy lawn. If you plan to raise the sail from its bag, you should first locate the head —that's the corner with the swivel—and the clews. Now feed the sail into the bag in a reasonably orderly fashion, beginning with the middle and making sure that each luff stays more or less at one side of the bag. (If one luff is color-coded, it's easier to keep them apart.) When it's done, you should have the three corners protruding. Tie the bag drawstring through the grommets so you don't lose them.

A spinnaker turtle is a type of bag which is made to attach either to deck fittings or to a bow pulpit. Its mouth opens more widely than a standard bag's, and there are two light snaps or Velcro closures at points across the mouth, so the head and clew corners can protrude separately.

To set a spinnaker in stops, spread it out and then gather it lengthwise in accordion pleats till it forms a well-compressed tubelike shape. Using heavy cotton thread or very light string, tie off the sail at intervals of a few feet, the spacing becoming wider toward the head of the sail. Take the stopped sail and bag it, starting with the middle and leaving the ends showing. This arrangement will allow you to make fast sheets and halyard before releasing the spinnaker.

The most frequent cause of public embarrassment with a chute is the crew's failure to lead both sheets from their turning blocks forward and *outside everything*—standing rigging, stanchions and lifelines and pulpit and other running rigging. Check the sheet leads after the lines are rigged, then check again before snapping them to the clews. If you drop the chute and then raise it again, recheck the leade before you do so.

Check also that the spinnaker halyard is running freely and that it, too, is led outside everything. This is doubly important if you normally dead-end the halyard to the bow pulpit: It is impossible (I have tried) to raise a chute through a pulpit.

Now rig the pole at the height you anticipate you'll want it to be when the sail is up. This is only approximate, even for experts, but a good rule of thumb is that the pole

One way of quick-releasing the spinnaker halyard (or any other tensioned line) is with this lever cam cleat made by Nashmarine. Thanks to the lever, it's possible to ease tension instead of just popping the halyard free. Personally, I wouldn't put a stopper knot in a spinnaker halyard.

should be high off the wind and somewhat lower reaching and in light airs. But again, the best pole position will only become apparent when the sail is up and drawing.

With the hands in the cockpit standing by sheet and guy, the halyard man takes the sail up fast—delay gets you nothing here. You can raise the spinnaker in the shadow of the main, or—and usually better for beginners—behind the jib. The chute should go up easily, and the sheet and guy tenders take in on their lines as the sail rises. This is important, because by separating the lower corners, you keep the sail from indulging in twists.

Raise the sail as high as it will go at first —you may want to slack off on the halyard, but that's a lot easier than trying to sweat up the spinnaker when it's begun to draw. Don't jam the spinnaker halyard snap into the sheave of the block, however—not only do you want to get the sail down easily when you're done with it, but you also want to be sure that the head swivel is free to turn.

Pulling the tack and clew apart may fill the sail and will (if you used stops) break it out. If the sail remains dead, trim in the jib or drop it entirely, and that will certainly fill the chute. Before doing this, however, make sure the halyard and the sheet and guy are all secured with at least a full turn (but not hitch) around cleat or winch. That first tug in a brisk wind can yank the hand on the halyard several feet in the air, if he isn't prepared.

With the boat on course, now comes the fun. The spinnaker is a symmetrical sail, and under most conditions it should set that way. If it's distorted to one side or the other, something is probably wrong. There will usually be major trimming in the first few minutes after hoisting, as the boat gains speed and the wind moves forward. Spinnaker trim is an art that distills the requirements of normal sheet handling. If you want to get the most from a chute, you have to keep handling the lines all the time.

In a good breeze, a crew of four is needed to get the most from the chute: One at the helm, one each for sheet and guy, and one forward to call the sail—he's the only one who can see all of it.

On the other hand, it's possible to overtrim the spinnaker so you can sail without touching it for hours, except in a major wind shift, but for the moment, let's concentrate on sailing the boat right.

The spinnaker is aimed from side to side and up and down with its control lines, two of which also act to change its shape. The sail's angle to the wind is adjusted primarily with the guy and secondarily with the sheet. Its shape can be made fuller or flatter by raising or lowering of the pole, or by trimming or easing the sheet. The sail's thrust can be directed up or down, to a degree, by taking in or easing the halyard.

The first principle of handling a spinnaker is that the sheet should be eased until the luff begins to curl, but stopped short of collapse. (For easygoing spinnaker sailing, just overtrim the sheet—you lose some efficiency, but gain peace.) The pole should be more or less

73

level with the foredeck, and at the same height above the deck as the clew of the chute. Thus the sail's free corner establishes the pole height. The pole is normally at right angles to the apparent wind. On a reach, judge this direction from the masthead vane, but when running, use the shroud or backstay telltales. If your boat has a high mast and a three-quarter rig, the apparent wind at the masthead may be markedly further aft than it is down at chute level—experiment will tell.

Once you have managed to get the spinnaker up and drawing well, you can try some finer points of trim. Two things to bear in mind continually are, first, that the main and spinnaker (and headsail, too) are a combination: trimming one will affect the other or both others. Second, the chute is in nearly all rigs the most important downwind sail: if it's necessary to starve one or another sail to feed wind to the spinnaker, then that's the proper thing to do.

Running is normally not a great problem in trimming, unless the boat begins a series of rhythmic rolls, which can increase until the spinnaker collapses or the main boom drags in the water and causes a broach. Since this type of downwind rolling is definitely self-feeding, the thing to do as noted earlier is simply change the boat's direction slightly. This action should break the rhythm. If the rolling doesn't seem to have a rhythmic pattern, then you can respond to it by squaring the pole and easing the sheet as you roll to windward; ease the pole and trim the sheet as the boat rolls back.

Reaching, especially with a jib set, the spinnaker tack should be somewhat higher than the clew. You want to open the slot between spinnaker and jib and ease the luff. There's a lot of sail interacting in such a situation, and you want to keep the sails free of each other as much as you can. Be prepared to sacrifice the jib if you have to, if it's a question of maximizing the spinnaker's pull. In

Occasionally, when reaching with a spinnaker in light airs you can point up a bit higher by dropping the outboard end of the pole to straighten the sail's luff.

medium winds, you can ease the chute halyard slightly when reaching, but don't do it in heavy winds, when it can lead to a broach, nor in light airs, when it can cause the sail to fold up.

To straighten a persistently curling luff, move the sheet lead forward of the transom.

If you do trim the spinnaker by using the halyard, remember that you've got the boat's biggest and most uncontrollable sail at the other end of the line. Always keep a turn around a winch drum or cleat, or you may be in for a nasty surprise. In gusty winds, you may choose deliberately to reduce the spinnaker's efficiency by overtrimming the sheet and easing the pole. In light airs, it may pay to lower the pole but keep the outer end cocked slightly up. You should probably have available a set of ultralight sheets, for use with drifter or spinnaker: 1/8'' braided flag halyard is about the lightest thing there is, although it's murder on the hands and will not activate some large cam or jaw cleats. In ghosting conditions, however, a light sheet can mean the

On the edge of too much: The crew of this San Juan 26 have all the wind their starcut can handle and maybe more; what they seem to be running out of is water.

difference between the spinnaker's holding it's clew up and maintaining shape, and the clew's dragging the whole sail down because of the weight of sheet and snap fitting.

The question of when to set the chute and when not is a hard one to answer. Racers generally feel that if you *can* hoist a spinnaker, you ought to, because even with an occasional broach, the boat will get to the mark faster than another vessel sailing more safely under genoa. Nonracers and skippers with small crews will of course feel differently. My own feeling, for what it's worth, is that in a breeze strong enough to make you think about replacing the largest genoa, you shouldn't attempt a spinnaker unless you have three adult-size, trained crewmembers besides the helmsman. Reaching, the first

75

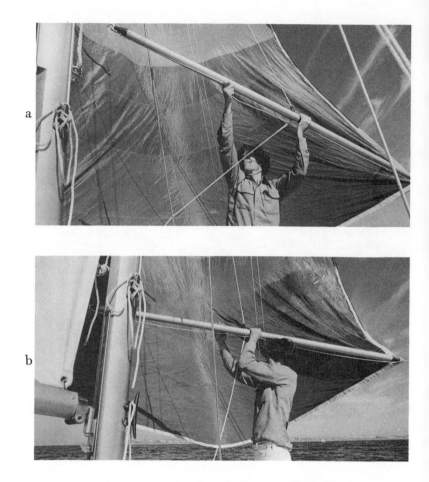

a

b

broach is as good a warning as you're likely to get: head off downwind or take the chute down.

If raising the spinnaker is the number-one crisis moment, retrieving it is probably number two. In my experience, most problems are caused by an improper lead to the spinnaker halyard block: The sail jams up, with the halyard bound against the forestay, or worse yet, as the sail is lowered, it streams out to leeward and then jams halfway down. Either condition can be embarrassing and dangerous, and the immediate thing to do is get the wind out of the sail while maintaining at least one downward control. Let the guy run out through the block and then head off, if the halyard's jammed. The change of lead should free the line enough to get the sail down.

Ordinarily, dropping the spinnaker should constitute no great problem. There are three ways of getting a chute down—by blanketing it behind the genoa, by taking it in behind the main, and by lowering it to windward.

In the first case, raise the genoa, or if it's already up change your heading till the chute collapses behind it. As the halyard man eases off on his line, one hand slacks the guy while the sheet trimmer scoops in the sail under the foot of the jib, being careful to keep it out of the water.

Without a jib, secure the spinnaker sheet forward of the lee shrouds. As the halyard and guy are simultaneously eased, gather in the sail. Don't let the guy run, but if it gets away from you, head off so the sail can stream downwind, not fall in the water alongside.

c

d

Taking the chute down to windward, simply unhook the pole and pull the sail around with the old guy as the boat heads up, then ease the halyard and drop the chute down on deck.

It's sometimes necessary to jibe the spinnaker, and while this situation arises more frequently in racing, it can happen aboard the cruising boat that is sailing a generally downwind course while piloting point-to-point. There are two basic kinds of spinnaker jibes—the end-for-end swap, and the dip-pole, pretty accurately described by their names.

In the first, assuming your boat is running, the foredeck man unsnaps the mast end of the pole, leaving the outer jaw still snapped to the guy. He then holds the pole athwartships and

John Breault of Hirondelle West jibing the chute aboard his own boat. The foreguy has already been taken around the inner headstay, and John unsnaps the pole, pivots the free end out, and snaps the jaws around the sheet. Then he unsnaps the other end of the pole from what is now the sheet and makes it fast to the ring on the forward side of the mast. This last step is often the most difficult.

reaches out to grab the sheet, bringing it in and snapping the pole jaw around it, then detaches the jaw at the old tack and makes it fast to the mast track. Finally, he shifts the pole foreguy to the new outer end. If the cockpit crew manages a smooth, easy jibe with

77

On larger boats, a single-ended pole with a bell-like outer fitting is often used in dip-pole jibes. A pair of lines lead through the length of the pole, and one end is shackled to each of the spinnaker clews. Jibing technique is shown in these illustrations from the Nicro-Fico people, who make this specialized hardware. (a) Slack off pole topping lift and line snapped to spinnaker tack. As pole drops (b), take in on line snapped to spinnaker clew (port corner, in this case) and pole lift. Pole swings inside forestay (c) and back up to new spinnaker tack (d).

no sudden lurches, the timing of the spinnaker changeover is not that critical. Ideally the pole shift should take about as much time as it does to get in the mainsheet, let the sail go over, and steady up on the new heading.

On the rare occasions when you may have to jibe from a reach, detach the pole completely before the jibe, and hook it up to the guy and then to the mast immediately after the jibe is completed. The cockpit hands will have to be on their toes to keep the sail full while all this is happening, but with good timing and smooth execution, it can be done.

The dip-pole jibe requires that the guy end of the pole be unsnapped, dipped under the forestay, and reconnected to the new tack. It requires a clear foredeck and no inner head stay even to attempt this maneuver, but it can be quicker and slicker than the end-for-end jibe. The difficulty can arise in trapping the new guy into the jaws of the pole, without disconnecting it from the mast. On many boats where the dip-pole jibe is standard, the spinnaker pole has only one jaw end, and the other is semipermanently attached to a specialized socket fitting on the mast track.

Other light sails are frequently used in connection with the spinnaker, especially by racers. The most frequently seen for many years was the spinnaker staysail, a nylon jib of weight approximating that of the chute itself. It was raised with the jib halyard or from a spare halyard about two-thirds the way up the mast, and it was tacked down well aft of the jib tack. The purpose, of course, was to utilize some of that wind that was escaping under the spinnaker foot.

Recently skippers have taken to using a high, narrow sail variously known as a tallboy or a splinter. It sets more or less athwartships (depending on the boat's heading), and may be tacked well up on the windward deck. Its

c

d

purpose is more to regulate the flow of air around the spinnaker and main than to provide a great deal of drive itself.

As mains have become smaller, their driving power downwind has decreased proportionately. With the size of the spinnaker regulated by rule and by common sense, it was clearly necessary to find something to replace the main on the leeward side when running. Cruising people have for years used twin jibs, poled out on either side of the bow, or even twin spinnakers, but this was for some time out of bounds. The most recent technique for racers involves the use of yet another specialized sail called a blooper or shooter. Shaped more or less like a fat banana, the blooper is tacked and halyarded like the genoa, but its sheet is led through a block near the end of the main boom and thence to the cockpit. It has no snaps along the luff, and sets flying.

Because the mainsail will normally keep a blooper from filling properly, the main is dropped all or part way. Effective as it may be, the blooper is a perfect example of a rule-created sail. Those skippers not restrained by the North American Yacht Racing Union can achieve much the same effect with a light genoa or drifter, extended to leeward by a whisker pole. If the main gets in the way, kill it—it's far the smallest of the three sails you have to choose among.

Ketches and yawls come into their own off the wind. To windward, a mizzen contributes nothing or less than nothing. Reaching, on the other hand, permits use of a mizzen staysail, a lightweight nylon triangle that is often as big as the main or larger. It sets from the mizzen masthead, sheets through the end of the mizzen boom and back to the cockpit, and is tacked down to a pad eye on the windward side deck, nearly abreast of the mainmast.

Although it is very large, the mizzen staysail is easy to trim, easy to raise, and easiest of all to lower—it falls right into the boat. The only problems with trimming this sail come when the regular mizzen blankets it. You may be able, by easing the staysail halyard and sheet or overtrimming the mizzen itself, to make the two sails compatible. In many cases, however, it will be simpler to furl the mizzen partially or entirely.

In this connection, it might be a good moment to point out that ketches and yawls make far less use of the mizzen as a balancing sail than they might. Regardless of the kind of reefing gear on the main boom, I feel that

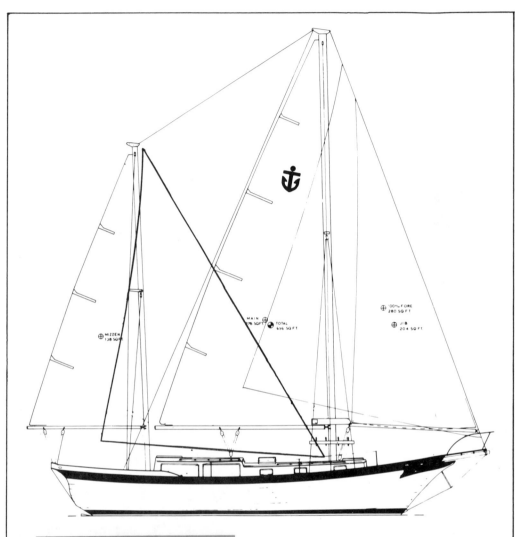

MIZZEN
138 SQ FT

MAIN
378 SQ FT

TOTAL
696 SQ FT

100% FORE
280 SQ FT

JIB
204 SQ FT

The mizzen staysail on this Down East 38 is 344 square feet—the largest sail on the boat, 40 square feet larger than the reaching genoa.

The same design, but rigged as a staysail schooner. The striped fisherman staysail is 185 square feet to the main's 241. A gollywobbler staysail, extending the fisherman down almost to deck level, would be close to 500 square feet.

roller reefing on the mizzen of a ketch or a yawl with a largeish mizzen is well worth the investment, as it allows sail reductions to be very carefully made, and thus makes the most use of the second mast.

11. Sailing in Close Quarters

Any fool can sail a boat in open water without getting into serious trouble, and many do. But sailing under control in close quarters is as much an expert's accomplishment as hitting the start line in clear air just as the gun goes off. It is, further, something which fewer and fewer people have given thought to. For one thing, auxiliary engines are now so universal on all but the smallest sailboats that it's a matter of moments to fire up the outboard and chug into or out of the harbor. For another, more and more harbors are becoming far too crowded to sail in safely—some harbormasters, indeed, have forbidden sailing in and around marinas or anchorages.

The fact remains, however, that a complete

Racers like these 110s have no choice but to learn how to handle their boats close to one another (Phil Acker photo).

sailor knows how to get someplace under sail if it's at all possible, and the only way to know how is to practice. (The complete sailor recognizes impossibility when he sees it, and that condition may become apparent as we continue.)

Most of the time, the trick to sailing under control in a tight place is sailing slow. *Slow* is of course a relative term, and for the sake of this argument, take it to mean slow over the bottom. There are times when you may have to move your boat quite quickly through the water in order to inch ahead in, say, a river with a strong current.

Close-hauled, there are several ways you can keep the boat from moving too fast, and each has its advantages and drawbacks, depending on the boat and the circumstances. Perhaps this is the parenthetical moment to suggest, too, that before one can sail a boat with good control, one must know it or its type well enough to predict performance accurately. If you're a guest on a strange vessel and

81

someone invites you to supervise the approach to the pier, you have every right to express a qualm or six.

Reduced sail is frequently the best method of reducing speed. It's especially good when you're aboard a boat that handles well under main alone, and you want a nice, clear foredeck for handling ground tackle. More modern boats often handle badly under main alone, and a jib works better—in a masthead sloop with the spar well amidships, the boat will probably point nearly as well under jib as under jib and main, and a good deal better than under main alone. She will usually foot faster and come about more quickly. If you cut a corner too close, a jib often produces less of a shambles than a main boom.

You will, however, sacrifice a certain amount of maneuverability when you unbalance the boat so radically. It's often better in light and medium winds to reduce the driving power of a sail by luffing, while retaining it hoisted in case you need it. Which sail you choose to luff when beating will depend somewhat on how your boat balances, but normally it's easier to luff the main slightly, while at the same time keeping it under control with the boom. When you're in a tight corner, a thunderously flapping jib does nothing to help you concentrate on the problem at hand and it can be unpleasant for anyone you've stationed on the foredeck.

If the situation permits, you can also remove much of the boat's drive simply by pinching up into the wind. The trouble with this as a maneuver is that sailing very close to the wind results not only in decreased forward speed, but also in a considerable increase in leeway, and a crablike course is somewhat harder to predict than a straight one.

Finally, you can sail an ordinary close-hauled course, occasionally heading up into a luff, then falling off to gain speed again. This is useful if you need to edge up to the windward side of a narrow channel. It works better

with long, slender, heavy hulls that retain their momentum than it does with light, shoal draft or beamy craft, which can be stopped all too easily. Centerboard boats that pivot quickly are not generally successful with this kind of trick—you can easily find yourself through the eye of the wind and off on the other tack.

When reaching, the options for reduced sail or luffing are also available. There can, in very constricted areas, be a problem luffing the main, in that the boom must be so far out to leeward that it can smash something. It may be better to overtrim the jib till it backwinds the main or is (on a broad reach) itself blanketed by the mainsail.

Running down into a narrow harbor these days requires nerves of steel and an accurate knowledge of what you're likely to find once you're inside. I recall the case, not too long ago, of a sloop that came into our own small anchorage basin on a dead run, boom all the way out to starboard. Too late the skipper realized that there was no room to swing up into the wind, and no room to jibe either. He edged further and further to starboard, trying to make room for a quick swing to port, up into the wind, until his boom collided with the outer shroud of a boat tied up at a float.

The result was spectacular. The docked vessel's rigging was completely wiped out, and her mast toppled slowly over toward the land, even as the running boat pivoted shoreward around the end of her own snagged boom and sank like an arrow into the pier. When I went home an hour later, the yelling had barely subsided.

If you have to run in close quarters, you can drop the main or jib, as before, but you can usually blanket the jib easily too. Perhaps the best way to cut your speed and minimize the dangers of an accidental jibe is by trimming the main well in toward the centerline. The only time you should have qualms about this tactic is when the wind is blowing strongly, and the shoreline is such that it can funnel a sudden, thwartships gust at you. On days like that, you may be better off to round up outside the harbor, drop everything, and sail in under a small jib.

In most sailing texts, including a couple I've written myself, the approach to the mooring under sail is given as a picture book problem, stated in the classic harbor situation: not too many moorings, at respectable intervals, with all the boats neatly pointing up into the eye of the wind. The only problem is deciding whose stern you'll cut under to make the approach to your own buoy.

Fewer and fewer harbors offer this kind of mooring facility anymore. There just isn't room to let boats swing in a full circle around their single anchor. And the harbors which still have single-anchor moorings are very much more crowded than they used to be.

Increasingly common are the bow-and-stern mooring systems, in which boats are made fast to anchors fore and aft, usually with a lightweight floating pickup line running between the two buoys. Thin as the pickup may be, it is still strong enough to stop dead any attempt to sail over it, and since it's usually polypropylene, it floats or lies very near the surface.

More crowded anchorages, especially those run on a commercial basis, frequently set up long lines of bow and stern moorings, wherein one boat's bow mooring is stern mooring for the one ahead, and so forth. The effect of this arrangement is to create a series of long, narrow lanes which normally cannot be crossed, even when the boats occupying the moorings are out, because of the pickup line which effectively runs from one end of the buoy series to the other.

Since bow-and-stern moorings are normally oriented to the prevailing wind, it is sometimes possible to sail up or down a lane of moorings. Running out of a line of moorings is normally no great problem: The exact

procedure is discussed a bit later. Reaching can be more difficult, because when the wind is crosswise to lines of moorings, the larger boats are frequently blown sideways to a greater degree than the smaller ones.

Tidal effects in and around anchorages can be very annoying. In areas where there's a considerable tide, it's not unknown for some buoys to be totally submerged at high tide springs*, and for others to drift out of line at low tides.

The additional effect of shoreside structures may not be at all apparent until you're committed to a maneuver. It pays, upon entering a strange harbor, to be extra alert at the sight of high buildings along the shore to windward. And while you're at it, keep a weather eye out for kids swimming from anchored boats and loaded dinghies that pop abruptly out from behind other craft.

The best wind indicators, when available, are the masthead flies on anchored boats with spars as tall as yours or preferably somewhat shorter. The normal breeze indicators may not show at all on the crowded water's surface, but the telltales are still functioning—and, in this instance, registering true wind direction.

Generally speaking, if mooring under sail in a crowded anchorage is problematical, entering a slip the same way is very risky indeed. A marina distills the problems of the anchorage and throws in some extras, of which the least predictable is the helpful lounger. Most people at dockside are all too willing to take a line. It's what they do with it that hurts; powerboat people especially seem to feel that any line handed them must be snubbed off hard immediately.

It is based on gut feeling, but my own willingness to hand lines to strangers decreases geometrically with the fanciness of the yachting caps they are wearing. I will

continued on page 86

Springs is used here in its technical tidal sense, as being a full or new moon tide of exceptional range.

a

b

c

d

84

In California's monstrous Marina Del Rey, skippers learn how to land under sail, as these photos show. In the first series, a singlehander brings his Bristol 22 to a very neat berthing by the classic method of heading up under mainsail alone. This skipper's proficiency is indicated by the fact that no one aboard the boat next to his turns a hair. The roller-furling genoa makes the maneuver easier.

nearly always hand a line to a person in a knitted, navy-blue watchcap, and usually to someone in a floppy spinnaker hat. The only time I tossed a line to a character in one of those peaked caps with gold braid on the visor, he dug in both heels, braced himself, and yanked my bow sideways into a shattering collision with the float I was so nearly alongside. No, in almost every case, it is wiser to get the boat dead in the water where you want it, and then pass a line over.

About the only time I will attempt a slip under sail is when the wind is blowing right out of it, and even then I'm not happy about it. Besides, when you're in one of those huge marinas where the finger piers stretch away into the far horizon, there is all too much activity with dinks and garbage boats and the like.

How can you tell in advance what to expect in a harbor if you've never been there before? Well, the answer of course is that you cannot for sure, but there are a few clues free for the asking:

—Anything marked "Special Anchorage" on your chart is almost certain to be jammed during the boating season.
—Do not expect to be able to see the government marks in a constricted anchorage basin; they may be visible, but then again they may be screened by moored boats.
—Look for large buildings on the large-scale harbor chart. Sizable ones are usually marked.
—If you use a Small Craft folio-style chart, be especially wary on weekends of

places marked as fuel docks. Not only will there be a crowd of boats being fueled, but there will also be a moving group of vessels waiting to get at the pumps.
—Any harbor with a posted speed limit is likely to be crowded.
—Read, if you have time, both the *Coast Pilot* and any available cruise guide for information before you enter.

The chances of making a successful landing in a strange place, or for that matter in one you know well, are enhanced if you and the boat are ready to take advantage of any breaks that offer themselves. Drop the centerboard, if any, all the way. Before you're anywhere near the entrance to the basin or marina, lines should be ready bow and stern, and people to handle them, too. Fenders should be on deck ready to be made fast—I now carry, aboard my 23-foot sloop, the fenders I bought for my 30-foot ketch; they're oversize, but very comforting indeed.

The bow hand should have ready access to a boathook. Personally, I vastly prefer the telescoping kind that extends from 4 feet to about 8 feet—it can make a lot of bad approaches into good ones, in the hands of someone trained in its use. (And for heaven's sake, don't expect your hapless crew to know by intuition that the boathook extends.)

The dinghy, if you're towing one, should be cinched up short. If it's inflatable, you can pull its bow right up over your mother ship's transom. What you don't want is to extend your boat's turning length unnecessarily, nor, if you may have to use the engine, to have a dinghy rode that can be swallowed by the propeller at the crucial moment.

And finally, it doesn't hurt to have the anchor made up, on deck, with enough line flaked out so that you can get it over fast just in case. If something does go wrong in the narrow confines of a harbor—or the narrower

Docking under jib alone is less frequently seen, but it's a perfectly acceptable tactic. Notice how this skipper keeps his jib only partially filled during the approach.

confines of a channel—it's nice to be able to drop the hook and sort things out in some kind of order.

Everyone who knows how to sail knows how to approach a single mooring. All the elementary sailing books are full of diagrams showing approaches to windward and off a reach and, for the carefree, quick buttonhooks off a run. All that's necessary to add here is that the approach to a single mooring isn't as easy as it looks. A certain number of times you'll miss and have to bear off for another shot. Always leave yourself the room to swing off (after missing the buoy, you may not have enough way left to come about), and don't be afraid to abandon a shot for the buoy.

If the mooring is your own, and you have leave to rig it as you like, I recommend a pickup float attached with light line to the mooring loop itself. In most waters, securing the main mooring buoy is no problem, but snagging the barnacle- and weed-grown line can be disgusting and difficult. If you have to grope for a line attached to the underside of the buoy and sunk out of sight, put on a pair of painter's gloves before you do. (Presumably one person is still holding the buoy with the boathook while you do so.)

Sailing up to a bow-and-stern mooring can be either impossible or very easy. If you have any choice in the matter, try to arrange for a mooring in the outer line next to the channel, or at the very tail (leeward) end of an inner line. These are the only ones you can reach under sail a good proportion of the time. Trying to pinch up between two lines of boats aimed nearly into the eye of the prevailing wind is something that people attempt year after year. It is almost always a dismal, destructive failure, involving tangled spreaders, scarred topsides, and a lot of bad feelings. If you simply have to get up to a spot on the center of an inside line of connected moorings, and do it without an engine, your best bet is to drop all sail and work the boat up

hand over hand along the others. Inelegant, but you'll get there, and the people aboard the moored vessels will realize that you have a problem and aren't being an ass.

Before rounding up sharply for a speed-killing turn to such a mooring, take a quick look behind you. Powerboat skippers often operate in a profound ignorance of what a sailboat can and cannot do, and when you ease over to the leeward side of a channel before heading up, the guy behind you may take it as an invitation to pass.

Sailing up to a pier or float is easy if there's a side that's parallel to the wind direction, or nearly so. It seldom happens that the edge of a float is exactly in line with the wind direction, and you may have the choice of a headwind slightly off or slightly on. If your stay at the pier will be short, I'd opt for the side that will let you blow off when you leave; if you're planning to stay the night or longer, it can be somewhat easier to let the wind blow you in the last foot or so.

If no side is in line with the wind, you can pinch up to a float with no trouble. Sail at the boat's very slowest, and expect the wind to fall away short of the float if there's a high bank behind. If you have the crew, let one person handle the bowline and lead a second line forward from the stern cleat, outside of everything, with another hand who will jump ashore, move down the float a few yards, and haul your tail in.

The downwind landing, whether under power or sail, is excruciating. If the wind is not strong and the boat not large, fender the

Not everyone has a slip upwind, and certainly coming into a slip while off the wind is bound to be less neat. This skipper manages it well, however. He swings as far upwind as possible, drops the jib as the boat turns off toward her slip, then glides in dead slow with the crew ready to step ashore.

leeward side heavily (never count on dock padding) and reach slowly along the pier, luffing freely, till you're where you want to be. Head up slightly, then stop the boat's forward motion by backing the jib and stalling the rudder—putting the tiller over to leeward. As soon as the boat stops moving forward, let the jib fly.

In a strong wind, there's nothing for it but to anchor and let the boat ease down slowly—beam on, if you can balance her well enough, otherwise any way you can manage. Before you anchor, it's a good idea to buoy the hook, not only so you can retrieve it more easily, but also to warn other skippers of what you've done.

The departure from a single mooring is another of the classic situations, and one that's been done to death in beginning sail texts. Somewhat more taxing is sailing away shorthanded after raising the anchor. Not only do you have the foredeck hand up there, but there's also a good deal of wet anchor rode and the hook itself, often encased in horrible mud. One method that works well with a two-person crew is to preset and cleat the jib sheet on the side toward which you plan to sail off, so that the jib will fill to a reaching wind. The bow hand gets the anchor broken free, and signals this fact to the helm. The skipper puts the tiller over toward the cleated sheet, and in a second (or several, depending on the boat), she will begin to gather sternway and her stern will swing. As she comes broadside to the wind, the jib will fill and the helmsman straightens out the tiller. At this point, the boat should stop and begin to move ahead, and the mainsheet can be trimmed—by which time the foredeck hand should have the anchor and rode cleaned off and stowed.

Sailing out of a bow-and-stern line mooring is, of course, only possible in a reaching or running breeze if you're in an inside line. With the wind from the beam, remember that the boat will move sideways a bit before beginning to gather headway, and that pinching her up won't help: You'll need at least a boat length down to leeward. Be sure the centerboard is fully lowered. Raise main or jib, depending on the wind and the boat, and drop both bow and stern lines simultaneously, as the sail is trimmed very quickly. One thing to bear in mind if you use a pickup line is that it must be on the windward side of the boat—you may have to untie it and lead it around.

Running off is easier. Raise the jib and let it stream away forward. Cast off the bow line and let the boat swing. When she is angled clear of the pickup line and the buoys ahead, cast off the stern and sheet in the jib. The wind will seldom be directly astern, so the bow should swing to one side of the mooring line, but even if the breeze is right over the transom, the boat should still weathercock slightly, and all you have to do is wait for the moment when she is headed right.

Sailing off a pier or float is no problem when the wind is offshore. It's usually better, though, to cast off the bow first and let it swing clear before releasing the stern line. In this connection, it may be worth mentioning a very elementary trick known by too few people: when you're sailing away from a pier, and you want to release your own line (not the pier management's) at the last possible second, simply pass it completely around the dock fitting and back to the boat; release one end and pull in the other. Simple and effective.

This is notably useful when you're alongside a float and headed right into the wind. Raising your best close-hauled sail combination, reduce your lines to a stern spring and a bow breast, as shown. Cast off the bow line and sheet in the jib—not too hard. Your bow will swing away, at which point you release the doubled stern line and sail off, to the gratifying amazement of any powerboat skippers standing by. You can, if necessary, swing the bow off even quicker by backing the

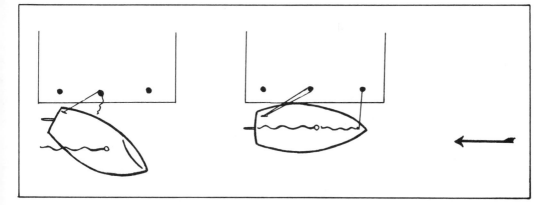

Sailing away from a pier can be a simple yet satisfying maneuver. The secret is in the doubled stern spring line, which allows the boat's bow to swing out; doubling the line permits you to retrieve it from the cockpit, without a man ashore.

but when sailing close to other craft, you ought to be generally aware of what happens when you sail into the shadow of their sails—and, for that matter, what your boat is doing to other sailboats nearby.

All sailboats create two kinds of wind disturbance as they move along. The obvious one

jib slightly, but it's usually not necessary.

Sailing out of a slip when your bow is downwind is just a variant on sailing away downwind from a bow and stern mooring. Normally I'd use a small jib to keep it from being snagged on the outer pilings, and release both stern lines at once. If you're bows-in at a slip, you may choose to try sailing out backwards. Raise your jib, or jib and main, and cast off the stern lines. When you're absolutely sure that there are no surprises outside the slip itself—an extra lookout ashore isn't a bad precaution—back the jib and cast off the bow. You may not move exactly backwards—this is a trick that warrants a good deal of practice—but you should be able to get the sail to do the work while the crew fends off.

Earlier in this chapter I've talked about the blanketing effects of buildings. When you're sailing in company with other boats, they exert a similar effect on your sailing wind, sometimes at a considerable distance. Normally only racers worry greatly about blanketing and dirty wind from neighboring vessels,

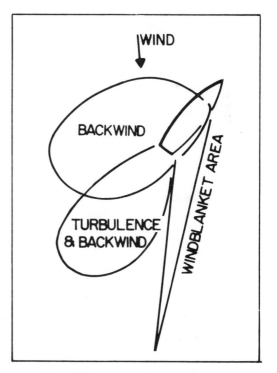

The several foul-air areas around a sailboat going to windward. The distance that blanket, turbulence or backwind will affect other boats depends on wind strength.

is a blanket—the blocking of wind downstream. The effective distance of a wind blanket varies greatly according to wind strength and the size of the blanketing sail. A group of boats together at a start line can create a collective blanket that affects other vessels well down to leeward of them.

Going downwind, a sail's blanket stretches more or less directly ahead, the effects diminishing at the sides of the blanketed area for several boat lengths. Beating, the blanket is to leeward, but eddies of disturbed air trail off directly aft as well. The faster a boat is moving, the more the bad air blanket trails aft. But a boat that heads up and attempts to pass to windward of another will frequently run into a similar eddying condition on the upwind side of the boat being passed.

Part of the reason for this apparent violation of common sense is that the windward boat's blanket is dragging well aft of her bows while under way. But even more important is the backwinding effect of the leeward boat's sails—currents of eddying air that swirl upwind and aft from the sails. This backwind stretches back in the same kind of triangular shape as does the blanket, matching it to create a wide cone extending to both windward and leeward quarters when a boat is close-hauled.

You can see the way this works yourself by sailing directly across the wakes of a tight group of sailboats working to windward—the area of obviously disturbed wind will extend not only down to leeward but also a considerable distance upwind as well. Coming off the wind, the blanket and the backwind effects merge, until the point where the blanket is the only one that remains.

Wind aside, sailboats often get into trouble dealing with the right of way conferred by the rules of the nautical road. A survey of experienced sailing skippers taken not long ago revealed that only about one in six really understood the rules of the road. Anyone who has ever seen a group of sailboats at night will appreciate instantly that very few of the skippers involved have any idea of what lights they should be showing or why.

So although this is not a book for beginners, it seems important to spend a little time explaining the rules of the road in detail as they apply to sailing craft. To begin with, there are at least two sailing right-of-way systems that may apply to any sailor, if he is racing. Between sailboats which are formally racing, the right-of-way rules of the United States Yacht Racing Union, or other national authority, apply even if the two boats aren't in the same race. These rules replace, by explicit agreement, the normal rules of the road for the duration of the race, with two very important exceptions.

First, the racing rules only apply to racing boats. When a racer encounters another vessel which isn't racing, the normal right-of-way rule—not the racing rule—is applicable. (And how do you tell a racer from a nonracer? Good question. If in doubt, ask, "Are you racing?" If the other boat is in a race and you're not, it is good manners to pass well clear to leeward of him.) Second, offshore racers normally use racing rules during the day and revert to normal right-of-way rules between sunset and sunrise.

Racing rules are incredibly complex and have no place in a book like this. If you're a racer, you should know the USYRU rule, which is basically the code of rules promulgated by the International Yacht Racing Union. There are a number of good explanations of the racing rules, several of which are listed at the end of this book.

In the United States, three different sets of right-of-way rules apply to inland and coastal waters, and there is also the International Rule to consider offshore. Unfortunately, local conditions that existed in past centuries have been frozen in legislative amber, so the several rules are similar but not identical, and there's the trouble. There is some hope that the Inland (read: *coastal*) and International systems will soon be brought closer to harmony, but this same hope has flickered on and off for years. And between these two systems is the greatest area of confusion, because in most coastal areas, only an arbitrary line drawn on a chart (but hardly visible on the water) divides Inland from International.

As a general rule of thumb, the waters which are legally covered by the Inland Rule consist of bays, harbors, sounds and the like. The line of demarcation runs from seaward headland to seaward headland, across harbor mouths. A complete description, point to point along the coast, of the Inland-International dividing line is yours free for the asking, by writing for a copy of the Inland-International Rule of the Road (which you should have anyway); it is a booklet numbered CG-169 from any Coast Guard District Headquarters or by mail from Commandant (CMC), U. S. Coast Guard, Washington, DC 20226. If you live and sail on the Great Lakes, you can get from the same address the Great Lakes Rules of the Road (CG-172); if your boat sails the Mississippi or its tributaries, the one you want is Rules of the Road, Western Rivers (CG-184).

Probably (it's hard to be sure) more boats sail under the Inland Rule than any other, so let's look at it first. There are five right-of-way situations between sailing vessels considered, and the rule itself is written with needless complexity. It states (a) that a boat running free gives way to a boat sailing close-hauled; (b) if two close-hauled boats are converging on different tacks, port tack gives way to starboard; (c) when two boats are running on opposite tacks, port gives way to starboard; (d) when both are running free on the same tack, windward gives way to leeward (*windward* when running being the side opposite to that to which the boom is extended); and (e) "A vessel

which has the wind aft shall keep out of the way of the other vessel," which is as close to useless as a sentence can get.

What it boils down to, then, is that close hauled has right of way over a boat running; if this situation does not obtain, then starboard tack has right of way over port tack; and if neither of the foregoing is the case, then the windward boat gives way to the leeward boat. If you commit that sequence to memory, you should have a handle on the rule—close-hauled, starboard, leeward boats have the right of way.

And having the right of way is an obligation in itself, as some people fail to realize. The right-of-way craft—the *privileged* vessel—is required to maintain course and speed insofar as possible until the danger of collision is past, so that the skipper of the *burdened* vessel can figure out how best to keep out of the way.

The International Rule is different. Only two situations exist: "When each [of two converging vessels] has the wind on a different side, the vessel which has the wind on the port side shall keep out of the way of the other." In other words, starboard tack has right of way. And, "When both have the wind on the same side, the vessel which is to windward shall keep out of the way of the vessel which is to leeward." Leeward boat has right of way.

Nothing at all about close-hauled versus running. A clear, simple rule that anyone can understand. The problem arises, of course, when sailing near the invisible demarcation line. On the Inland side of it, a close-hauled boat on port tack would have right of way over a boat running on starboard tack. Once you cross into International Rules' jurisdiction, however, the right of way reverses.

Sailing rules for the Great Lakes are the same as the Inland Rule cited above, except that the meaningless section (e) is not included on the Lakes. Western Rivers Rules, which are more concerned with steam vessels in swift-running streams, follow the Inland

Rule for sailing craft.

With respect to other boats, sailing craft have the right of way over powerboats except when (1) the sailboat is overtaking the powerboat, (2) in a narrow channel, where the power vessel cannot navigate safely except in the channel, and (3) when approaching a commercial (not a private) craft engaged in fishing with nets, lines or trawls. Aside from the wording of the rule, sailors will do well to keep clear of larger powercraft as a matter of common sense. It may be wholly obvious to you that it's necessary to zigzag upwind while staying within the channel, but the powerboat skipper is likely to think you're just harassing him. The trouble is, he may be right. If you're tacking up your harbor, keep an eye out for powerboats closing you astern, and motion them on to pass when it's safe. Likewise, in crowded waters always look astern and to windward before you tack.

Keeping clear of commercial fishermen is usually easy; when fishing, they're stationary or moving very slowly. The only thing to bear in mind is that fishermen who are using nets may have a tremendous amount of line out; "clear" in relation to them may be several hundred yards. Ordinary fishermen are another situation entirely. It seldom occurs to them that a monofilament fishing line, designed to be invisible to a fish, is also invisible to sailors. If you don't see a line leading from a pole that is obviously in use, look down to leeward for a float or bobber. If you don't see *that* and you're a good 50 yards or so away, to hell with him.

Trolling boats, which casually trail a hundred yards or so of line from three or four rods, can also get in one's way. Often—and especially if the light is poor—you can't see the line and the wake hides the lure's splash. Slow-moving powerboats with attended fishing poles, or even a rod or two in sockets aft in the cockpit, are good to keep clear of, unless you are the sort of person who is stimulated by abuse. If you allow a good hundred yards astern of a trolling boat, you should be safe enough.

The several rules of the road are very precise about the kinds and conformation of running lights to be displayed in poor visibility by sailing craft. It's hard to understand why so few sailors show the proper lights at night unless they don't give a damn—and that may be the answer. One otherwise skilled skipper I know remarked to me that he turns on all his lights at night, so people can see him. The problem is that when he's done this, other captains don't know what it is they're looking at, or what they ought to expect it to do.

The lighting rules are intended to show three things: (a) that a vessel is there; (b) what kind of boat it is, in terms of its right-of-way obligations; (c) which way—approximately—it's heading. If you show the wrong lights, other skippers literally won't be able to tell if you're coming or going or standing still; or whether you're a sailing vessel they should keep clear of, or a powercraft over which they have right of way. The ensuing confusion may well create a collision situation where none existed before.

The types of lights to be displayed are shown in the accompanying charts, which speak for themselves. They speak a little louder if you take an hour or so to study them, and to imagine how each pattern would appear at night and at different angles. On some small cruisers, builders still wire all the running lights to one switch, so that you don't have the option of turning on power or sail displays, as the occasion warrants. If this is the case on your boat, you should change it at your first opportunity so that you can signal all three of the following situations: (1) under way under power (or power and sail—does your jib foot clear the side lights?); (2) under way under sail alone (and the same parenthetical question applies); (3) at anchor.

Powerboat skippers, more at home with the

Rules of the Road—Required Lights

(A) Sail alone: Note that a boat under 40 feet in International waters *may* show a combination bow light, but all vessels in Inland waters, and those over 40 feet in International waters, *must* show separate red and green side lights when under sail alone.

comb 20 pts 1 mi   10 pts 2 mi

(B) Power alone or sail and power: International waters (also usable on Inland waters, including Great Lakes and Western Rivers). Boats between 40 and 65 feet must carry the 20-point light nine feet above the gunwale, as well as three feet higher than the red and green lights.

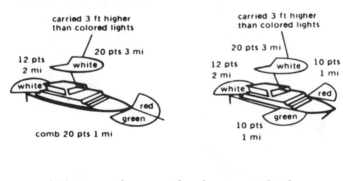

(C) Power alone or sail and power: Inland waters, including Great Lakes and Western Rivers.

LESS THAN 26 FEET   26 FEET TO NOT MORE THAN 65 FEET

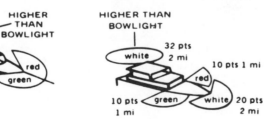

95

vagaries of electricity afloat, know that running lights often don't work when you switch them on. It's usually only a matter of wiggling the bulb in the socket—but make it a part of your standard night-running drill to check each light after you turn it on. A 20-point powering light on the forward side of the mast may be screened from below, but it will usually glint off the stays and will always show against the jib. A masthead light should have enough upward glow to illuminate the burgee or wind vane, once the sun is fully down.

12. Advanced Anchoring

It sometimes seems to me that what makes effective anchoring so hard is that the concept of it is so simple: all you do is tie a string to a hook, drop it over the side, hook the bottom, and there you are. There you are, that is, momentarily. The idea is simple, the execution somewhat less so.

If an instructor were to leave one abiding feeling about anchors with his student, it would probably be: *never trust them*. There

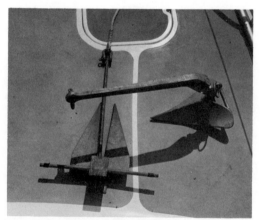

Danforth (left) and CQR Plow are certainly the most popular anchor styles aboard modern sailboats. Though it may not seem so, Plow is much heavier: 15 lbs. to 8.

will be situations all your boating life where you have no choice but to rely on your anchor, but there should always remain that nagging doubt in the back of your mind, not enough to spoil your fun going ashore, but at a sufficient intensity so you always check the rode before you go, and a sudden wind change ashore will send you back to the harbor to see that the boat is riding safely.

Questions about anchoring always begin with *what kind* and *how big*. The two queries are related, of course. These days, it seems to me that most sailing skippers I've seen go for either the Danforth or the Plow.* A cadre of salts holds out still for one of several varieties of the ancient yachtsman's anchor—the conformation depending not only on quality, but also on the type of bottom that skipper usually encounters.

There are others, to be sure—folding grapnels, the Northill, mushrooms and the ever-surviving Navy stockless—but they seem to me either very specialized indeed or unsuited to sailing craft. For the average skipper, the choice will usually narrow down to Danforth or Plow, unless his anchorages are normally very rocky, in which case he may opt for the yachtsman shape, which is becoming increasingly hard to find at reasonable prices.

How big? I have always found the manufacturers' size charts quite adequate, and I include three of the standard ones here. The problem, of course, is that length is not an accurate way of describing a boat. Most of these charts were worked up when sailboats were longer, narrower and deeper than they are today—heavier, but offering less windage at anchor. Once dug in, an anchor will usually

*I include in these designations the various imitators of each basic design, although I do feel there's a qualitative difference between the original of a thing and its copy. Impartial tests on the Plow—made in England—have shown that the CQR variety is demonstrably better than most of its less costly copies. (I suspect the same is true of the Danforth, although I have no figures to prove it.)

TABLE OF SUGGESTED ANCHOR SIZES
Anchor weight in pounds, normal conditions

Boat length	Danforth	CQR Plow	Yachts-man's
under 17'	4	5	10
17-20'	8	10	12-15
20-25'	8	15	15-20
25-30'	13	15	25
30-40'	22	20	30-35

(For storm anchor, take one size larger in each instance.)

stay put unless jerked out by a great increase of force or an abrupt change in the direction of pull. So if your boat is a plunger (like most catboats and others with the masts well forward) or if she habitually sails around her anchor, I would suggest one weight heavier across the board.

If the quality of the bottom where you sail is generally firm—sand or gritty mud—either the Danforth or the Plow should do well. If there is significant weed growth, the Plow may be better, but if it's kelp—long, tough streamers several inches wide—nothing is going to be too successful. In soft mud the Danforth or the Plow will hold if they can get down far enough, but in gravel or small shells few anchors are reliable. For rocks or coral, the yachtsman's comes into its own, although many skippers are turning to the folding grapnel, which has at last become boat-broken.

The anchor is about two-thirds of the

ANCHOR RODE SIZES, NYLON LINE

Boat length	Rode diameter	Rode Circumference	Strength
to 14'	5/16"	1"	2,850
14-20'	3/8"	1⅛"	4,000
21-25'	7/16"	1¼"	5,500
26-30'	½"	1½"	8,350
30-40'	5/8"	2"	12,000

equation, the rest being the rode. For effectiveness, nothing beats chain, which also adds significantly to the weight of the rig—and to the weight you have to raise and lower. Chain also scars the gunwales of most boats unmercifully, and a serious quantity of it can put even a large craft down by the head. Personally, I don't see it, except for a length up to 10 feet long between the anchor and the rode, for added holding power and chafe resistance where chafe is most likely to be a factor.

There's nothing like nylon rode for an anchor—it's one of the rare instances where a substance meets a requirement almost to perfection. The abbreviated chart shows the sizes of line I personally would suggest, and it's worth adding that these sizes are so heavy for smaller boats not because of any added strain but because line lighter than about 3/8" is pure murder to haul in by hand after the first 50 feet or so.

How many anchors? Anywhere from one to three, depending on the boat. Daysailers don't need more than one, weekending cruisers can get away with a light and a storm anchor, but the serious cruising skipper will probably want a very light one for fishing or other brief halts, a medium-size working anchor for most overnight occasions, and a storm anchor. I've always carried both Plows and Danforths, and if I sailed in rock strewn waters, I'd probably stow a yachtsman's too, with a rode for each.

Anchor stowage is a perennial problem, but one that has been solved for years across the water, where European and British builders mold self-draining anchor wells into the foredeck as a matter of course. Without such a convenience, one has the choice of keeping the working anchor on deck, where it will sooner or later snag a line—usually a sheet in the middle of a tack or jibe—and rip its chocks free, or keep it in a locker, where it will be covered by the other things you've stuffed in afterwards. Although it may seem a waste of space, the working anchor's stowage place should offer maximum accessibility of anchor and rode, and be for them only: no other lines or fenders or life jackets or whatever.

Locker aside, the second (or 22nd) best place is probably on the foredeck, chocked down with the rode led below to the inevitable locker in the eyes of the boat—unless you are fortunate enough to have a bowsprit, in which case the anchor finds a natural resting place under it. Bowsprits are so very useful in this connection that not a few cruising boat skippers have added them simply to have something from which to suspend a Plow anchor in the ready position (because of its shape, a Plow is perhaps the least stowable of the popular anchors).

Anchors, chain leader, rodes—what else should your anchoring system include? At the risk of belaboring the obvious, you'll require shackles as connectors between rode and chain and anchor. Be sure that the shackles are strong enough to do the job, according to the table shown. You'll also want to eye-splice your rode around a thimble and wire the shackle pin so it cannot back off. If you anchor in rocky ground a lot, it may pay you to carry aboard a small buoy or float (a plastic detergent bottle with molded in handle is

WORKING LOADS OF GROUND TACKLE ELEMENTS*

Rode (nylon) Diam/Load	Chain (galv.) Diam/Load	Shackle (galv.) Size/Load
5⁄16″/570 lbs.	3⁄16″/1,400 lbs.	3⁄16″/670 lbs.
3⁄8″/800 lbs.	same	1⁄4″/1,000 lbs.
7⁄16″/1,100 lbs.	same	5⁄16″/1,500 lbs.
1⁄2″/1,670 lbs.	1⁄4″/4,350 lbs.	3⁄8″/2,000 lbs.
5⁄8″/2,400 lbs.	same	7⁄16″/3,000 lbs.

*Working load of rope is 1⁄5 breaking strength; Working load of chain is 1⁄2 breaking strength; Working load of shackle is 1⁄6 minimum strength, and nominal shackle size is 1⁄16″ less than pin diameter.

ideal) and 40 or 50 feet of 1/8″ flag halyard to make a tripline arrangement. Most larger anchors have an eye fitting up near the crown for just such a rig. If the anchor snags, you can pull it out backwards, rather than trying to sail it out.

I don't think much of the weights that some people run down along the rode to flatten the angle of the line relative to the bottom. Theoretically, such a device (consisting of a chunk of lead suspended from a saddlelike messenger that slides along the rode, and a light retrieving line) should improve the anchor's holding power. In practice, I have the feeling that you could wind up with an unholy tangle and some unlooked-for chafe in the bargain.

Sea anchors are another controversial subject—just about as many experienced voyagers abominate them as swear by them. You have to take your choice. A sea anchor is supposed to hold your boat's bow or stern into the wind, while keeping the boat from sliding down to leeward too fast. Most coastal sailors don't have that kind of leeward to play with anyway. If you own a cruising boat, before investing in a sea anchor see what the owners of other boats with hulls like yours have to say about them.

If you do decide that one will work for you, don't skimp—get a large size (which means diameter), of heavy, nonrotting material. It will spend most of its life in a dark locker, and when you need it, you want more than a rusty steel ring and a handful of fat moths. The open-end variety seems to be generally more successful, and the trip line used in connection with powerboat drogues is probably more of a complication than an asset. In my experience, two lines close enough to tangle invariably do so.

The techniques of anchoring under sail are normally not difficult. The mistakes usually made are two: first, the anchor is likely to be tossed in before the boat has any sternway, so the first few feet of rode land atop the hook —an invitation to fouling. Second, sailboat skippers seldom plant the anchor firmly enough. With Danforth and similar anchors, this can result in fouling later, if the stock (the crosspiece on which the flukes are mounted) isn't fully buried and the wind or current changes. If you use the engine for nothing else all day, it will pay to sock it into reverse just to bury the anchor fully with about 3-1 scope. Then ease off to 5-1 and you should ride nicely.

There may be an occasion when you have to anchor bow-and-stern, though this is not a desirable maneuver if you're planning to leave the boat for any length of time. Should the wind direction change 90°, you can impose considerable strains on the anchors. Normally, you would anchor with the bow facing into what is or will be the direction of greatest stress. Taking the longer of your lines forward (if it isn't there already), you drop the large anchor and fall back to the end of the rode, at which point you lower the smaller anchor. Pull about halfway between them and use the engine to set first one, then the other.

If you expect the principal force (wind or current) to come later from what is now downwind, run the long anchor rode outside all the rigging to a stern cleat, then drop the heavy anchor off the bow and let the boat drop back to let go the second anchor. When both are in, you can swing the vessel to present her stern to the large hook. If possible, remove or retract your rudder if you anchor stern to the current or waves. Nonremovable rudders should have the tillers lashed amidships with shock cord—not regular line—so the rudder blade stays centered, yet has some give if the boat swings and the water strikes it at an angle.

If a storm is predicted and you want to lay two anchors, it's a good idea to put them out in a V-shape from the bow. Get both anchors and rodes ready while close-hauled, with the longer rode on the leeward side or the foredeck. As the helmsman calls *Hard alee* and the bow comes round, the anchor with the long rode goes over. The boat is put on a beam reach at a bit more than right angles to the waves (if that is the direction from which the storm winds are predicted to come). At a signal from the foredeck man that the long rode is nearly gone, the helmsman rounds up and the other anchor goes over. Trim the two anchor lines till you have the boat at the apex of an angle of approximately 50 to 60°, with one anchor line somewhat shorter than the other: If the storm is strong enough so the anchors get dragged into a straight line, at least they won't foul.

In normal conditions, when mild night winds and/or a tidal change can be expected, anchoring to two hooks is an invitation to a horrible tangle: The boat will almost certainly swivel around several times, and perhaps swivel back later, not untangling the original snarl, but only complicating it. This is a point to remember if you raft up with another vessel overnight: use his anchor or yours, not both.

Sailing an anchor free is a maneuver that requires a good deal of confidence on the skipper's part and, preferably, a boat which will handle well under mainsail alone. The foredeck hand will have enough to do without being distracted by a flapping jib. With the sail raised, slack off on the anchor rode and put the tiller over till the boat falls off on a close reach; as she gains speed, bring her up to a beat on the same tack, while the foredeck crew takes in the rode as quickly as possible.

As the boat comes abreast of the anchor, snub off the rode. The anchor should pull free, possibly jerking the bow around on the other tack. Bring the anchor aboard quickly but carefully, so as not to scar up the topsides with the flukes. If the anchor is encased in mud, the crew will have to souse it off the bow, holding it away from the hull as best he can.

One of the keys to sailing the anchor out successfully is to come up alongside the bedded anchor as close as possible. To do this when there's a lot of rode out, you may have to sheer well off to one side, then come about and beat directly at the anchor. Except in large boats, where getting the anchor in without a winch can be a trial, sailing the hook free is at best a satisfying trick—but then so are most sailing maneuvers beyond the basic ones.

About the only anchor system that can give me peace of mind is a proper mooring, which is reasonable when you stop to consider how much of the boating season you'll spend attached to it. More and more harbors give discretion to officials—marina owners or harbormasters—in the supervising of mooring rigs, and this may be just as well, except that far too few of today's harbormasters either know or care much about their jobs.

There's no reason you can't calculate and assemble your own mooring rig, according to the table shown here. Like all anchoring tables, it has to be approximate. If you anchor in a location exposed to the prevailing wind and the seas driven by it, use the next higher weight of anchor and rode. If you use bow-and-stern moorings, deduct one third from the weight of the anchor: The two-thirds remaining will be the weight of *each* of your two anchors. Finally, don't interpolate: go to the next higher weight for security's sake.

The location of your mooring should offer the same attributes as a good anchorage—protection from seas in most directions, including that of the prevailing fair- and foul-weather winds; accessibility to shore and supplies, without too much traffic; and the presence of neighboring boats taller and more visibly luxurious than yours (for built-in protection from lightning and thieves, respectively). The bottom, assuming you use a mushroom anchor, should be soft, deep mud by choice. Given time, a mushroom will work its way into most reasonably soft bottoms, but it may take a while.

SUGGESTED SIZE OF MOORING RIG COMPONENTS

Boat length	Anchor (lbs.)	Chain°	Shackle	Pennant°
to 16'	75	3/16"	1/4"	3/8"
17'-20'	100	1/4"	5/16"	7/16"-1/2"
20'-25'	150	5/16"	3/8"	1/2"
25'-30'	200	3/8"	1/2"	5/8"
30'-40'	250-300	7/16"	1/2"	3/4"

°Chain length should be twice maximum anchorage depth; Pennant length should be as long as convenient, but no less than about 15 feet. Mooring buoy must be able to support the weight of chain lifted off the bottom, and should not normally take direct pull of the boat to the anchor—e.g. shackle the pennant direct to the chain. A buoy of 12" diameter, filled with polyethylene foam, will support 24 feet of 3/16" chain or 15 feet of ¼" chain; a 16-inch diameter buoy will support up to 35 feet of ⅜" chain. An 18-inch buoy will hold up about 60 feet of ⅜" chain.

Shackles should, of course, be wired and all metals in the system should be compatible galvanically. The nylon pennant should be oversize in diameter in case the chafing gear wears through during a storm. I once incurred a good deal of amusement among my friends by using 1/2'' nylon as the pennant on a 17-foot catboat's mooring. The laughing stopped one morning after a severe storm when the bow chock was found to have sawed its way through the chafing gear and through one strand of the line. The boat, unlike some others, was still there.

As to chafing gear, there are two precautions you should take before affixing it. First, make sure the total diameter of line and chafe protection will fit into your boat's chocks. Second, double check where the chafe will come when the pennant is under real stress. Put the engine in full reverse, and you'll probably find that the line will stretch several inches between the deck cleat and the chocks. The chafe gear should be arranged to absorb punishment in both fair weather and highly stressed situations.

The spliced loop in the end of the mooring pennant should be a large one—big enough to put twice over the deck cleat without forcing. Obviously, the cleat itself should be equally large. I won't discuss the backing a mooring cleat should have, but if you have any doubts, take the line around the cleat and then lead it aft to the mast, just in case.

If you use two buoys and a pickup line between them, polypropylene (or one of the other floating lines) is the obvious choice. To make the line easier to see—and less likely to be run down by others—it doesn't hurt to tie in a float every three feet or so. The pickup line itself will be run from one pennant loop to the other, so that hooking the pickup line at any point will give you possession of both pennants.

Single-anchor moorings can also make use of the small pickup float in additon to the main buoy. The light float is often fitted with a vertical fiberglass pole, so it can be grabbed by hand from the foredeck. If your nylon rode is long enough, you may not need a main buoy at all.

Moorings should be inspected at least once a year. For some reason I don't understand, the critical corrosion point in a given mooring may be at any one of several places, often at the point where the chain encounters the surface of the bottom mud. If you don't want to pull the mooring, you can probably hire a diver to check it out for you. Or if the anchorage is not too deep, cold, or malodorous, do it yourself.

13. Surfing and Planing

Back toward the beginning of this book, we made the distinction between displacement and planing as kinds of motion through the water, and looked at the basic hull types suitable for each. Briefly, the displacement hull, which always moves through the water, functions best when it is designed to disturb the water flow least; on the other hand, the planing boat, which is supposed to skim across the surface, requires a hull shape that will be easily supported by the water.

It should be borne in mind, however, that almost any kind of hull can escape from its own wave system and plane, given enough power. Sailboats don't ordinarily plane because the power isn't available from the wind, and they aren't usually equipped with large enough engines to make planing under power possible in a sailing hull. Under certain circumstances, standard displacement craft —even ones of considerable size—can be in-duced to plane momentarily, assisted by sea conditions.

This kind of sailing is called *surfing*, and it happens, as a rule, only in strong winds and short, steep seas. In surfing conditions, the boat is often very nearly out of control, and a wild broach is not an unusual way of ending the ride. Still, surfing is éxhilarating and, in a good boat, not dangerous. The essence of surfing is that the boat, driven at or near hull speed by strong winds, picks up an extra increment of speed from a wave and is hurled forward, breaking briefly out of the displacement mode. The surfing ride lasts as long as the boat can hold her place on the wave—not more than half a minute as a general rule.

By contrast, a planing boat may require only an instant of surfing—or none at all—to enable her to ride up and over the forward wave of her self-created wave system. She is then light enough and her rig is powerful enough for her to maintain position more or less atop the water as long as the wind remains strong enough to move her at planing speed. Planing is not only exciting; it is also much more controllable than surfing and it offers a quantum increase in speed.

Like anything else in boating, you have to pay for it by having the right kind of craft and the right kind of equipment, and a boat ideally suited to planing under sail isn't very well adapted for anything else. Boats which surf readily are, in hull form, usually not far from planing craft themselves: they normally have a rather fine entry, with bows sharp at the waterline (and often flaring above, for extra buoyancy). Aft, the hull is flat bottomed or nearly so, and quite beamy, to offer maximum support for the crew. With few exceptions, keel boats do not plane, although they can surf easily enough. As one might expect, planing hulls sail with centerboards mostly retracted when at top speeds.

Some of the new breed of offshore racers can surf for so long that the difference between what they're doing and planing is only academic. For the most part, these are vessels with centerboards or retractable keels, their hulls like oversized dinghies. For most cruising boats, planing is not really desirable because of the sacrifices in comfort and accommodation which would have to be made, and because in the waters where most cruisers operate, there simply isn't enough wind, enough of the time.

Surfing is another story. Generally speaking, you need seas steep enough and large enough so the boat can actually ride the forward side of them while completely supported by a single wave. The movable weights should be well aft, and the boat trimmed for running.

In fact, the best surfing is usually done on a broad reach, with the hull at a slight angle off dead downwind. As the seas come up from astern, pick a likely one, fairly steep and large, and start the boat directly down it. If you begin to surf—and the sensation is unmistakable—head up a bit and trim the sheets immediately, as the apparent wind will move forward instantly.

The boat's bow will have a strong tendency to dive, and people in the cockpit will probably be sprayed by sheets of water. Steering is tricky, not only because of the distraction, but also because the rudder will lift and become less effective. If you're in a centerboarder, the board should of course be nearly all the way up, with just enough fin showing for some directional stability amidships. Your rudder will be under extreme strain, and if you have any doubts about its construction, if it seems at all loose in the fittings, better not attempt surfing at all.

Roaring diagonally down the seas, the boat may suddenly broach—swing out of control up into the wind. This can be more unnerving than it is dangerous, but it's serious all the same. Broaching most often occurs when a boat is on too much of a reach, and the initial tendency has to be caught immediately, with helm and eased mainsheet. If the boat goes all the way around, she should right herself if she is a keel boat or a keel-centerboard cruiser. In serious conditions—and the wind to surf a cruiser is by definition serious—hatches should be kept shut as a matter of course, and every sheet should be tended.

Running in surfing conditions with a spinnaker is not for the beginner or even the advanced novice. If you're bound to make knots, however, the chute will provide them, keeping your average speed made good between surfings much higher than for the boat which loses speed drastically after each wave ride and then has to make it up again. Both main and spinnaker must be rigged with extreme care, and the crew should (in a boat of any size) wear life vests and harnesses.

The mainsail should be flat down, with the vang leading slightly forward to act as a preventer in case of a jibe. The spinnaker, which should be a star-cut type or a flat, small-shouldered storm variety, should be raised in stops. Carry the pole with the outboard end down and overtrim the spinnaker sheet. In these conditions, it's a good idea to double both sheet and guy, leading the unused (or *lazy*) line forward to stabilize the corners of the sail.

Don't try reaching with the chute in surfing conditions—it's asking for a broach. Run nearly ahead of the seas. When it's time to retrieve the chute, it's usually best to let the guy run right out through the block and through the pole, and then pull the sail in under the main boom with the lazy sheet. Jibing, too, is needlessly hazardous. Drop the chute entirely, jibe the main, then reset the spinnaker on the other tack. Should a knockdown occur, ease the spinnaker sheet and the mainsail vang to bring the boat up on her feet, then head off and retrim the sails.

On occasion in running during heavy weather, you may be pooped. A wave may break from astern when your boat is in the trough and roll right down into the cockpit. If you don't have a large cockpit, and if the access below is sealed off, being pooped is a good deal more noise than danger. And noisy it is. The oncoming roller makes a sound like a train, quite audible over the cacophony aboard, and as it towers over you, the wave seems twice its true size.

For smaller vessels, pooping is really a special case of surfing. Your boat will suddenly be screaming off with the wave, while the cockpit is full of water. The important thing is to keep the craft headed straight—she will be unstable with all the extra water in her—and get the cockpit bailed as quickly as you can: With the boat sluggish and the stern down, a second pooping could break against the main hatch slides or doors and flood you.

Planing a daysailer is perhaps more restful, since if the boat does go over, little or no harm should be done. Generally speaking, boats designed for it can begin to plane in winds of 10-12 knots or so—Beaufort Force 4. Light-weather planing is like surfing, in that it's occasional, and a plane will usually depend on a gust, and end when the puff does. For skippers new to sailing a planing hull, this kind of wind is best for the first few shots, as it allows one to absorb the sensations of planing while having time to catch one's breath.

Begin on a beam reach, with the boat level in the water, both fore-and-aft and athwartships, and the crew amidships. The boat should be moving at her best displacement speed, with sails correctly trimmed to that speed and the centerboard nearly (but not quite) all the way up.

Now watch for the telltale water signs of a puff: the dark patch of close-textured ripples racing across the surface, or boats abeam and to windward suddenly heeling. Bear away slightly just before the puff arrives, and as the boat picks up speed, head back up to the original course, while trimming in the sails quickly. Keep the boat sailing flat by hiking out if necessary.

If you've got enough wind, the boat should become unstuck and climb over her own bow wave. Move the crew aft to keep the boat at a slightly bows-up attitude. This can be tricky, and it takes time and practice to work out the best angle of attack for the hull: With the bow too high, the boat will be safe and stable, but the transom will bury and drag you back. Bows too low, so that the boat is sailing on her narrow forward sections, and you may broach as the rudder lifts.

As you pick up more speed, sheets will have to be trimmed still further to compensate for the apparent wind moving ahead. As the puff dies, head up slightly to keep the apparent wind speed as long as you can before coming off the plane, at which point you can ease sheets in response to the drop in speed.

As wind strength increases, it becomes easier to get up on plane and easier to hold it

Even small children like these have no trouble righting a lightweight sloop, though they may have to combine their weight. The kids are students in the Norwalk, CT Small Craft Program, and the boat is a Zef.

for extended periods. You may be able to plane on a close reach with no effort at all. Once up, of course, you must pay close attention to the boat's trim and to the sheets.

The same principles still apply in strong winds, but they apply faster. The crew should be well aft and will probably be hiked out with feet under straps. The objective is still to sail the boat nearly flat, and in strong gusts this may not be possible by crew weight alone. In a heavy puff, head off, not up, to reduce the apparent wind speed. At the same time you can ease the mainsheet slightly.

Planing attitude of the hull becomes more important and harder to control. The bow may have to ride a bit higher, at the sacrifice of some speed, in order to avoid a sudden broach off a wave, or even running the boat right under. If the bow drops suddenly, the crew may save the day by letting the jib sheet run, thus taking pressure off the forward end of the boat.

As much of a danger, with both the crew hiking at full stretch, is the windward capsize, when a gust dies abruptly. The only thing to do is head up instantly and trim both the sheets. Trimming sheets while hiked out is a problem, and most helmsmen use one hand and their teeth alternately when large amounts of sheet have to be taken in fast. Otherwise, you can trim by holding the sheet with your arm slightly bent, retaining a little adjustment either way—for continual trimming of both sheets while planing is vital.

Strong winds, if they blow long enough over a great enough distance, will produce sizable waves. In a small, planing daysailer, sizable may be a couple of feet high—not enough to bother with aboard a cruiser, but quite enough to take account of in a small boat. Planing through waves is a special case of surfing, and it's necessary to alter course continually to get the most from the waves when you're riding them, while slowing down as little as possible when you're between rides.

What this amounts to is a continual shift from beam to broad reach and back again. You reach up the back, or windward, side of the wave using the wind alone, waiting for a puff to accelerate your boat enough to catch up with the crest. As the bow breaks through, you pick up the extra speed of the downhill slide, which you can prolong by sheeting in hard and heading up, till you're whizzing diagonally down the forward face at top speed. Once you lose that super speed, you fall off and ease sheets to begin your assault on the next wave ahead.

A refinement of planing is provided when your boat has trapeze gear. While a strong man or woman can hike out for some time with only thighs, calves and feet in the boat, a trapeze enables a sailor to get it all out, fully extended at right angles to the water, for maximum righting leverage. Extra leverage means the potential for carrying extra sail, which in turn means extra speed in a planing boat.

Trapeze gear will vary in detail, according to the ingenuity of the sailor and the rig of the boat, but it consists of the same essential parts. On either side of the boat, a wire is led down from the shroud tangs. At the end of the wire is a grab handle of some sort and under it a line and light tackle for making length adjustments—as when changing to a different-size crew. At the lowest end of the rig is a ring, often of a design that allows for ultrafast additional lengthening of the whole affair. This ring slips into the hook on the forward side of a harness worn by the crewmember. Padded somewhat behind, the harness goes over both shoulders and through the crotch, although the main stress is taken on the band across the seat.

Properly adjusted, the trapeze should allow the wearer to extend at right angles to the boat, supported under the buttocks, with the grab handle within easy reach. If the water is flat, the crewmember can use the ring at extended length, which brings him lower to the surface. If it's rough, or if the wind is such that the hand has to swing frequently in and out, he'll usually set the ring at the raised position. A length of shock cord is often made fast between ring and boat to hold the gear in when it's not in use.

The crewmember is normally seated on the gunwale far enough aft so the trapeze wire will pull him forward. For that reason, it's important to push out with the forward foot, to keep from being swung ahead. On the trapeze, lock the forward knee and keep the aft one bent enough to counter the forward pull of the wire. With practice, you can move fore and aft as well as extending or retracting your righting effect by straightening or crouching.

Getting back in may be a reverse of pushing out, or you may simply lift both feet off the gunwale and swing in to land on your seat. Remember, however, that any movement will alter the trim of the jib, whose sheet must be eased or taken in to correspond with the action of the crew holding it. In time, it's even possible to tack with the crew swinging in, unhooking, slipping under the boom as the boat comes about, hooking up on the new windward side and pushing off as the sails fill.

This kind of thing is not for the untrained, nor for those in only average condition. Trapeze hands should always wear shoes and life jackets, whatever else they have on—many of them find that wet suits conserve body heat and provide adequate buoyancy. Sailing gloves are another useful accessory. Conditioning for hiking or trapeze work consists of the normal exercises for strengthening stomach muscles, such as situps, with or without the toes hooked under something. Running and bike riding, to strengthen leg muscles for long periods of partial crouching, are also good. You can kill two birds (and maybe yourself, too) by running with a couple of five-pound dumbbells.

A lot of work, yes, but a great many sailors find the effort well worth it.

14. The Sailboat Under Power

Since few powerboat hulls perform adequately under sail, it's perhaps only fair that most sailboats make unfortunate powercraft. Not only are sailboat hulls less than perfectly suited to being driven by propeller, but most

A common sight, seen every summer day when the wind is wrong, but what does the skipper do if his engine quits? With an onshore wind and no sail ready to hoist, he could be set down on that jetty before he had a chance to sort things out.

sailboat engines are auxiliary installations, in the dictionary sense—too small to do a good job, sited where they will interfere least with other things, pushing propellers that are a compromise between drive and drag.

Even so, nearly every skipper of a nonracing sailboat bigger than a dinghy considers equipping his craft with some sort of engine, and most of them wind up doing so. For boats under about 25 feet overall, an outboard is almost always the most sensible choice; from 25 to about 30 feet, the choice between outboard and inboard power is a toss-up; and boats over 30 feet are nearly always equipped with inboard power, more and more of it diesel.

These are not, I hasten to add, invariable rules: I have owned a 17-foot cabin catboat that performed very well with a single-cylinder inboard and a three-bladed propeller; and only a week before writing this, I encountered a 40-foot catamaran driven through a calm by a 25-horsepower outboard with a double long shaft. Both of these vessels were unusual in their auxiliary power, however, and the average skipper, while realizing that alternatives exist, is usually better off adopting an orthodox, well-tried solution to the engine problem, once it's been determined that an engine is necessary at all.

And that's a point in itself, even though few Americans can imagine a boat without an engine. Not long ago, I ran across a small, cuddy-cabin sloop—a classic Herreshoff design reproduced in fiberglass. She had no outboard mount, but on the aft outer corners of her cabin were an unmistakable pair of oarlock sockets. Intrigued, I asked the owner how come, and he replied that after a year or two with a dud motor he had lost patience and flung it overboard, to replace it with a couple of sweeps, which he rowed standing up, facing forward. When not in use, the oars broke down into two pieces and were stowed under the floor boards. For working into and out of

harbors, he claimed, the arrangement was quite successful.

Not many modern sailboats are at all well shaped for rowing, and decked boats can be very difficult to paddle for any distance. In small craft, the owner usually falls back on an outboard. To the question, "How big an engine do I need?" the initial response (not really stalling) is, "What do you want it for?" That is, if you need a kicker to spare you that last half-mile up the creek to the anchorage, your requirements will be considerably more modest than if you plan to use it for bashing the same boat several hours into headwinds and seas.

For small boats up to 15 feet or so, the smallest outboards (well, not the *very* smallest) should be enough—4 to 6 horsepower, weighing 30 to 60 pounds. Engines of this size should bring the boat to near hull speed, they are relatively easy on fuel, and they're light enough so that it shouldn't be too much of a struggle to strike them below.

Boats of the larger daysailer size will be able to handle a bit more horsepower, though they probably don't really need to have it. What they do need is a proper propeller, which may or may not be the standard one sold with the engine. If the boat isn't able, in calm water, to work up to hull speed after a full couple of minutes on a straight course, check with the dealer. Optional propellers are now available to match the engine motor to the job.

When one gets up to the small cruiser, the whole situation immediately becomes more complicated. Nearly all daysailers carry the engine mounted on a bracket through-bolted to the transom. The outboard can be tilted up—either by itself or by raising the bracket and then tilting the engine—so the propeller clears the water when sailing, a most important feature. But while some small cruising boats have transom cutouts for the engine, others have wells, and some still limp along with transom brackets.

a

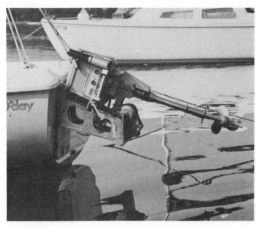

b

c

d

e

Here are a number of ways of mounting an outboard on a sailboat. (a) Non-folding bracket is unsightly and places engine weight way aft, but the engine can swing up clear of the water; (b) More usual outboard cutout—but the motor swings right into the cockpit with you; (c) This bracket slides up and down in a track, so a long-shaft motor isn't required; (d) A bracket that swings down, mounted on the extreme port quarter of a catboat—but not quite high enough; (e) Desperate remedy, a quintuple-long-shaft outboard in a well aboard a 37-foot catamaran; the line helps retract the motor for sailing.

My own feeling is that there are several things one should require of an auxiliary engine on a cruiser, where it serves a much more important purpose than a kicker on a daysailer. First, it should supply maximum drive, which usually means a three-blade propeller; second, it should be accessible but not obtrusive—you should be able to reach all the controls and even clean a spark plug without assuming a position similar to ones seen in erotic Indian wall carvings; third, it should—hell, it *must*—be fully retractable when sailing; fourth, it must be reliable without fuss; fifth, it should be capable of recharging the boat's storage batteries while underway; sixth, its compartments (running and stowage, if they are different) should be capable of being ventilated according to Coast Guard requirements without a lot of difficulty; and finally, it should provide adequate range under power for at least a half-day's run.

Happily, outboard engine manufacturers have responded quite well to these needs in the last few years, and there are now available two sizes of engine—approximately 10 and 15 horsepower, respectively—which fill four of the criteria listed above (the other three have to do with the installation, which depends on the boat). These engines, manufactured by Chrysler for several years, and now joined by Johnson and Evinrude, are designed for the job of pushing displacement hulls, which means both lower gear ratios and different props than are usually provided for outboard engines.

They come in manual and electric-start versions, with a low but still useful generating capacity—enough to offset the demands of running and cabin lights and a bit more, which is usually enough on small cruisers. With the standard six-gallon detachable tank, they will provide four or more hours' running full tilt, which can be easily extended by carrying a small emergency tank (something one should

do anyway). If I sound enthusiastic, I am. The engines are still noisier than most inboards, but they seem to me significantly quieter than outboards of only a few years back.

The installation of this paragon may be easy or complicated, depending on how well your boat has been designed to receive it. The reader may have noticed that I said nothing about being able to steer the outboard in my list of requirements: That attribute, which is so important on ordinary outboard equipped vessels, is very often something one must surrender in sailboat installations. Reverse—yes, definitely; but you should be prepared to steer with the boat's tiller.

Some outboard wells are placed on the centerline, right aft of the rudder. Since it's very difficult to put an outboard forward of the rudder, this is probably as good for general steering as you're likely to get, but it usually entails a sealed well, which is hard to fill with the fresh air necessary to keep the motor going. An ideal outboard well should be open at the front as well as the bottom, for ventilation and for access to the controls—the gear lever is usually at the side, while the speed control and start-button/pull-cord are on the face.

You lose a small amount of efficiency by putting an outboard bracket or cutout to one side of the transom. Simply by angling the engine till the boat powers with a neutral helm, then screwing down on the engine's turn adjustment, it's possible to eliminate this problem. With a very wide transom, it may occasionally be an advantage to have the engine mounted at one corner, as this will permit very tight turns in one direction (and correspondingly less sharp ones in the other).

Shaft length is a critical adjustment, and while nearly all outboards provide a long shaft version for sailboat use, some have an additional length of shaft for installations where the motor must be clamped very high off the water. If the boat's wave form is such that you get a hollow at certain speeds where the propeller turns, you may very well be blessed with a serious cavitation problem, in which even a small wave will be enough to pull the propeller free of solid water and make it overwind madly. Before buying an engine, sail the boat at hull speed to see what the wave conformation at the obvious engine location will be. Off the transom, of course, the wave is likely to be high at near maximum displacement speed, but a well a bit further forward may be a different case.

Remember, in planning your installation, that both engine and fuel compartments, if they are separate, require Coast Guard-approved ventilation. This means either a compartment that is substantially open to the atmosphere, where no fumes can collect, or a ventilation system consisting of at least one intake and one exhaust vent: the intake tubing leads at least halfway down the compartment, and the exhaust tube is at the compartment's functional low point.

If the compartment coincides with the bilge, the lowest point will probably be the sump, but the bottom of the main bilge compartment will be a better termination, as the sump will from time to time be filled with water.

In boats from about 30 feet up, the inboard engine is a logical choice for most people. It provides generating capacity, better fuel economy, and (if you like) the safety of diesel power. Outboards of 15 horsepower or so weigh something like 75 pounds, not counting the extra heft of batteries and fuel, which will bring it to over 150. The smallest gasoline inboard, providing 7-horsepower on a single cylinder, weighs more, not including gasoline or battery, and the smallest diesel, a single-cylinder, 5-horsepower model, is nearly 200 pounds.

When you get to the more popular auxiliary inboards, you're up to 500 pounds and more with no effort at all, which means that the engine must sit more or less in the center of the boat and as low down as possible. You wouldn't like living in your own bilge a great deal, and the engine, also an air-breather, doesn't care for it, either. But modern marine engines, both inboard and outboard, are amazingly reliable, considering the lack of care they usually receive from the sailors who own and ignore them.

Were I shopping for an inboard auxiliary, I would look for several things—first, a good record of reliability; second, quiet operation; third, simplicity; fourth, a well-distributed dealer network and a good service record; and fifth, a good service manual. Sailboat people are, in my experience, quite open about their engines' performance and about the performance of the people who sell them. By asking around among skippers with boats more or less like your prospective purchase, you should have no trouble getting a reading. The dealer network need not be national, as long as it's where you are—and as long as parts don't have to come from the other end of the earth.

As for the choice between gasoline and diesel, I am inclined to be postjudiced (which is prejudice based on incomplete experience): I've never owned a diesel, but I've never had a happy experience aboard a boat that carried one; I also spent five good years as shipmate to an Atomic-Four, a gasoline engine which repaid neglect and dirty fuel with consistent, trustworthy performance. Many other people have had quite opposite experiences, with more to base them on.

Let's look at a few hard facts. Unless you use a diesel engine a great deal more than most sailors, you won't make back the extra cost in cheaper fuel and lower consumption. So the engine is more expensive. Engine weight of diesels in the smaller sizes is getting down to where it is at least comparable to gasoline engines, so that problem is not really critical any more. Diesels are said to be more reliable than gasoline engines, but there are probably more people who can repair gasoline engines, and the parts are more generally available. As is fuel.

What about the vital question of safety? Gasoline engines can blow you up, diesel engines generally won't. Although I once saw a gasoline-engined boat explode and burn within two yards of me, I have also seen a hell of a lot that didn't. I think this is a question that has got to be answered by you. Explosion does not get me nervous, whereas the smell of diesel is something I find peculiarly unpleasant. Nevertheless, I would have a hard time justifying an inboard gasoline engine for a family boat.

Racing sailors generally go for folding propellers, which are certainly less drag. I doubt that they are worth it for cruising skippers, but at the same time it is very important that you be able to lock your standard,

On a larger cruiser, a three-bladed wheel like this makes up in motoring efficiency what it sacrifices in sailing performance.

two-bladed wheel in an up-and-down position, preferably directly behind the keel. The normal, and easy, way to do this is by rotating the engine slowly at anchor someday, and noting when the prop is vertical. Now mark the propeller shaft with a scratch. If you can't see the shaft, try arranging a sight line down through one of the cockpit lockers, which usually go right down to the bilge.

By comparison to other boat-and-motor combinations, the auxiliary sailboat is usually underpowered, and turning an inefficient prop to boot. The result of this condition is that the boat takes a good while to work up to speed, and an equally long time to decelerate in response to reverse. This is the main point to keep in mind when bringing an auxiliary up to a mooring or pier under power: no brakes, and not even the satisfying burst of reverse to stop the boat in her tracks, as powerboat skippers do.

Power approaches simply have to be made at the slowest possible speed consistent with maneuverability. Going ahead, the inboard-powered sailboat will normally have a tendency to turn to port—someting that can be quite marked at high speeds. In reverse, she will have the same stubborn attribute, trying to pull her stern left.

You can make this work for you if you plan ahead. When approaching a pier or mooring, it's good practice to kill forward momentum by making a tight turn up to the desired spot. Your turns to port, in an inboard-powered auxiliary, will usually be perceptibly tighter than the turns to starboard. By putting the rudder over and then giving the engine a quick burst of speed, you can increase the sharpness of the turn. By the same token, when easing alongside a float, if you come in at a slight angle portside-to and give the ghosting vessel a shot of reverse, she should stop moving ahead and tuck her stern neatly into the pier—very effective, when you get the hang of it.

Starboard-side approaches, by contrast, can be messy. Even when you come in at a flat angle, reverse tends to kick the stern away from the desired place. On the other hand, you can frequently reverse away from a float if you're starboard-side to it, whereas it can be impossible when your port side is along the pier. In this situation, run a spring aft from the bow to a point on the dock amidships, and go slow ahead till you lever the stern out, then reverse.

Backing out from slips can be a nightmare in auxiliaries, especially when the wind is blowing you back in. The boat may steer as well as she does going forward, she may not steer at all, or she may sheer uncontrollably in one direction (usually, but not predictably, to port). The best thing to do is practice the maneuver over and over again, using as little rudder as possible. With the rudder ahead of the prop, as it usually is on an inboard auxiliary in reverse, the wash tends to yank the rudder all the way around to a stalled, nonfunctional angle.

Backing clear with an outboard auxiliary, you can often steer reasonably well if you can turn the engine even slightly one way or the other. But beware of the altered pivot point: going backwards, the boat is very likely to spin around a point quite near the stern, which means that you'll be flinging more than half of your craft from side to side as you turn.

Finally, and this is a point most powerboat skippers don't have to worry about, the sailor who turns on his engine should not only run the blower (if he has one) for the suggested five minutes—he should spend a couple of those minutes making sure that none of his many sheets and/or docklines is trailing over the side, ready to be sucked into the prop. The most likely time for such accidents is during the general milling about attendant upon dropping sails for the final chug up to the harbor under power. Running home, you're not so likely to be concerned with good

sail trim and where the sheets have gone as you are when you set out, and there are all too many ropes' ends that can easily escape over the side—not excepting the dinghy painter, which will usually wait till the last-minute burst of reverse to do you in.

Yet another reason to be able to sail up to the mooring.

15. In Heavy Weather

It's very seldom that severe weather conditions drop on you without warning. A slow deterioration is far more common, except perhaps on hot summer afternoons, when a thunder squall may come up to round off the day with a bang. By taking a little care, you can see the thunderstorm coming from far enough away so you can begin appropriate precautions well in advance. And with storms of sudden violence, you may take heart from the old (and true) weather jingle:

Long foretold, long last;

Little warning, soon past.

In the preliminary squall of a cold front, the winds may increase very fast—by 15 knots each minute, according to Alan Watts in *Wind and Sailing Boats*. Brief gusts to 60 knots are not beyond expectation, nor are hailstones of quite painful size. More dangerous are sudden changes in wind direction, often accompanying gusts—not to mention the unnerving effects of nearby thunder and lightning bombardment. Happily, such tempests seldom last more than an hour from first to last, and the serious part is generally over in half that time—not nearly long enough for serious waves to form, although you may be sprayed by a nasty little chop.

More enduring bad weather will almost always be heralded by warnings considerably in advance of its arrival. Although weather forecasts are quite often wrong, the error is usually on the side of safety—yours—since a storm cannot come from nowhere at all. The most tricky conditions are often those in which your boat is running before a gradually increasing wind and sea, under a gray but essentially featureless sky. Only when the wind shifts or your course changes do you become aware of just how much the wind has piped up and the seas risen.

The two keys to bad weather seamanship are preparation and simplicity. You must plan ahead what steps to take if you're caught out in serious conditions (and practice what you plan); and you should keep your preparations basic enough so you don't clutter the boat with a lot of vital bits and pieces which can never be found when you want them. Remember, too, that rolling in a practice reef on a sunny July afternoon with a 10-knot wind is a different order of effort from doing the same thing when it's gusting to 30, at the chill end of October, maybe in the dark.

Emergency operations, however cleverly conceived, have to be carried out in emergencies. Were it not for this fact, sailing would be a lot simpler and—to be honest —less interesting.

Getting a sailboat ready to face heavy weather involves several steps, none difficult. First, you and your crew should know what steps of sail reduction come in which order. This will depend to a great extent on the rig of your boat and on the wind direction. Let's look at a few sample possibilities.

Daysailing sloop: Ordinary working sail is the main and genoa/spinnaker. First sail reduction—reef main as far (if required) as lowest batten. Second sail reduction—shift to small jib, regardless of heading. Third sail reduction— remove jib or furl main, depending on heading, and boat's best performance. Finally—drop and securely furl all sail; heave to or run under bare mast.

The working jib on a San Juan 21 center-boarder is low cut to keep heeling down. The main is just on the verge of luffing and a reef will shortly be a good idea.

A rather hoky shot of a Dawson 26, but it does show that even a very small ketch can be both practical and attractive. Reaching under heavy-weather conditions, this jib-mizzen combination would probably be successful; going to windward the main and jib would most likely be more effective.

Traditional sloop: Ordinary working sail is large jib and main. First reduction —shift to smaller jib. Second reduction—tie in first reef in mainsail. Third reduction—lower small jib, set storm jib *or* tie in second reef, depending on boat's balance. Fourth reduction—perform whichever function was not done at time of third sail reduction. Final reduction—sail or heave to under double-reefed main.

Ketch: Ordinary working sail is genoa, main, jib (if on the wind); same less genoa, plus spinnaker and mizzen staysail off the wind. If beating, first reef, then drop mizzen; next, reduce size of headsail and reef main in alternate steps; end with fully reefed main. Off the wind, first drop mizzen, then replace spinnaker with small genoa; then remove mizzen staysail, followed by a reef in the main. Furl main and replace mizzen.

Two Vega 27s in really serious weather. The jibs seem to be doing most of the work.

End by sailing under fully reefed main or small jib, whichever provides best balance.

And these are not all the things one might do, or even the best. They are only obvious sequences that should work reasonably well in most boats of the types described. You must experiment with your own boat—but during a storm is not the best time. Ideally, you should choose a day with sufficient offshore wind so that you can operate in breeze strong enough to give a sense of sailing in heavy weather, while at the same time being close enough to shore so you can vary the intensity by sailing in or out. As a general rule, one effect that really strong winds will bring is a sizable increase in weather helm, most perceptible on reaches. This effect will be more pronounced the larger the main is relative to the foretriangle; catboats, with no foretriangle at all, are legendary hardmouths when reaching in a heavy breeze.

Your boat's mainsail (and mizzen, if you have one) reefing system is probably beyond your selection, except as one of the stock attributes of the boat. There are three systems around today, each with its advocates and detractors, and you can learn to live with any of them. The one found on older craft is the so-called *point reefing* arrangement, in which one or more rows of short lines set parallel to the boom are sewn through the sail. More modern, and perhaps most common, is *roller reefing*, by which one rolls the main around the boom, like a windowshade. The newest system—although it is really a version of the original method—is *jiffy* or *slab reefing*: grommets in the luff and leech of the main are pulled down to the boom with hooks. (The way each system works in practice is described later.)

In point reefing, separate, detachable lines are used to secure tack and clew reef points, and these lines have a habit of getting misplaced or used for something else. If you have point reefing, you should have an inviolate place for the tack and clew reefing lines, and a spare for the longer one. The vulnerable point in roller reefing is often the reef handle—the lever which rolls the boom. If it's removable, there is every chance it will sooner or later fly over the side. Not only should the original be equipped with a lanyard which can tie it to the sailor or the rigging, but you should also have a spare. Jiffy reefing tackle is both cumbersome and single-purpose, so it's not too likely to wind up in the wrong place. But tackles tangle easily when not set up, and yours should be stowed with care.

Speaking of stowage, there is nothing more disconcerting at the onset of bad weather than that first serious roll, which dislodges all the badly stowed gear and tosses it on the floorboards. Cabin boat or daysailer, everything which is not going to be used during the storm should be stuffed into lockers and padded with clothing or cushions if it's breakable or likely to break something else. Foul-weather equipment should be broken out and set up if possible. Items which may or may not be called for—the anchor is an obvious example—must be moved to a place where they can be reached easily, and lashed down so they will not cause damage.

This done, the boat can be sealed as well as possible. If it comes to the worst, you want to retain the watertight integrity of hull and cabin as long as possible. Hatches should be closed and dogged shut, ventilators sealed or trimmed away from the expected wind, cockpit and lazarette lockers accessible from on deck should be closed and latched. (The first thing a new boat owner should do is figure out how to seal out as much water as possible, and install the hardware to do it.)

If the weather seems very foreboding, it will not hurt to double-check the gear specifically set aside for emergencies: Are the flares handy and in a dry, accessible place (such as an extra-thick watertight plastic bag)?

Does the radio transmitter work? Is the man-overboard gear set up and ready to go? The life raft, if any, available?*

The skipper should have an overall plan always in mind when bad weather is hinted—for all-day or longer trips, he should have alternate destinations both up and downwind (an ideal situation, perhaps) at one-hour intervals. Now is the time to begin homing in on the plan, and telling the other people aboard what it is. It is a nice piece of communication to alert people to difficulty without scaring them unnecessarily, and in a modern, democratic society it takes perhaps more skill than it used to. One thing the owner of a boat can take comfort in—over and over, it's been proven that any plan, understood and practiced by the crew, is immeasurably better than none at all.

*I mean both self-inflating and manually inflated rafts, but not dinghies, which should be taken aboard and lashed upside down at the first warning of heavy weather. There is no way to test a self inflating raft without inflating it, but you may be able to blow up one compartment of a regular inflatable. without making it too unwieldy.

If the bad weather is near, the crew should put on foul weather gear and life jackets. Anyone who feels this step is overdramatizing can be reminded that it's a lot harder to get dry than to keep dry, and when the boat begins to leap about, a sailor's-style life vest (the type with foam padding all around the wearer's body from waist to neck) is great for cushioning bumps.

Boats in which the crew will have to work on deck should, of course, have lifelines and stanchions. They should also have a locker containing safety harnesses for the foredeck crew—I prefer harnesses sized to be worn outside of the life preserver and foul-weather jacket, so that if you go over the side, the shock of the line yanking you back to the boat will be cushioned somewhat by the life jacket's padding.

Finally, if time allows and the siege looks

A very intelligent pulpit-lifeline rig on a Danish offshore boat allows the genoa to set properly while retaining the upper line at maximum height for safety.

to be an extended one, some high-energy nibbles and a hot or cold drink (not booze) will bring the crew up to the mark. There will probably not be time or the inclination to eat once it gets really rough, not to mention the difficulty of operating the stove, if you have one. I usually tuck a well-wrapped fruit bar or some pieces of candy in a convenient pocket for later on, but those with less cast-iron stomachs will want to get their eating over with. Now is the last convenient call for the head and for seasick remedies, though a certain amount of delicacy is required to make either suggestion.

Reefing has been a fact of sailing life from the beginning, and the simplest kind of reef consists in reducing the functional (as opposed to the literal) area of the sails. Gaff riggers have an edge (one of their few) here, in that they can instantly reduce the effective size of the mainsail when off the wind by lowering the outer end of the gaff till it's roughly parallel with the boom, an operation called *scandalizing.* a Marconi-rigged boat can achieve the same effect if the vang is allowed to run and/or the topping lift taken up. In either case, it's a temporary measure for decreasing the power of a sudden gust.

The point reefing arrangement has been described over and over, and there's no need to dilate upon it here, except to suggest a couple of refinements. The keys to a well-tied reef are in the tack and clew lines, which must not only lash the sail tightly to the boom, but must also stretch its foot aft as taut as you can get it. The tack and clew reef lines go around the spar, as opposed to the reef points themselves, which go under the sail, between its foot and the boom. All the reef points should be tied at the same tension on the same side of the sail. If there is more than one row of points, beware of tying one of the deeper set into your first reef.

The furl of the reefed area isn't terribly important—it's nice to be neat, and a tight furl keeps the unused part of the foot out of the way, but what really counts is the evenness of the ties along the reef and the tautness of the new foot. Some skippers, who don't like rows of reef points flapping on the sail, remove them and leave only the grommeted holes. When a reef is needed, they lace a lightweight lanyard through the grommet and under the foot of the sail and back up through the next grommet, and so on. This provides a somewhat neater reef and a more even tension along the foot, at a slight cost in time.

While it's possible to sail along on a close reach with a little air in the top of the sail while you're tying in a reef, it's not easy, and the usual procedure is to drop the sail till the reef is in, then rehoist it. That's not necessary in roller reefing: The sail remains largely raised the whole time, although it is luffing.

Points to remember when rolling in a reef are these: you'll probably have to remove at least one luff slide or slug from the track or

Two problems of roller reefing are the easily-lost handle and the necessity to exert a pull aft along the foot of the sail to avoid the lumpy roll shown here.

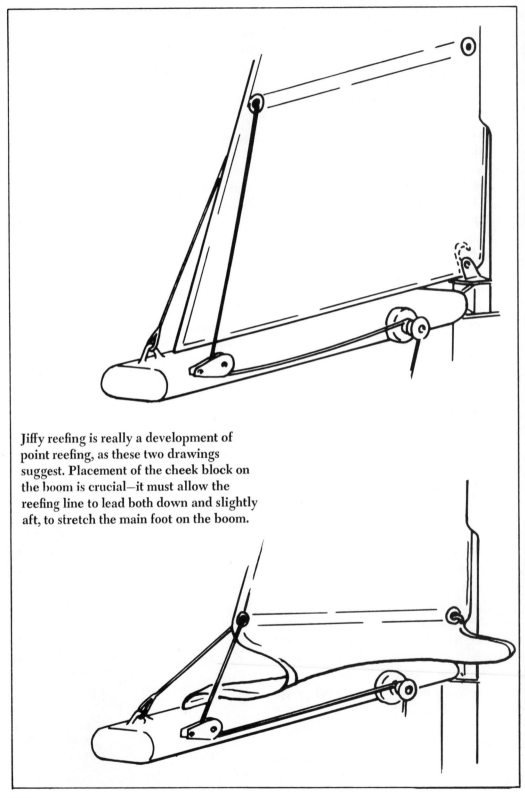

Jiffy reefing is really a development of
point reefing, as these two drawings
suggest. Placement of the cheek block on
the boom is crucial—it must allow the
reefing line to lead both down and slightly
aft, to stretch the main foot on the boom.

groove in order to take a reef of any size at all, and this will entail releasing the stop at the bottom of the sail track or the pin at the lower end of the groove. Do it before you start reefing. Maintain tension on the halyard while rolling in the reef—in fact, if your boat has a sliding gooseneck it's good practice to roll the boom up the sail, rather than slacking off on the halyard. Just keep enough tension on the gooseneck downhaul to ensure an even roll. At the same time, someone in the cockpit should be pulling the leech back along the boom, to minimize vertical wrinkles in the foot of the rolled sail. Be careful when you approach the lowest batten: if it lies along the boom, you may roll it right up in the sail, and if it's rolled at an angle, it will probably be destroyed. If you roll in a very deep reef, the boom will probably droop at its aft end. If this begins to happen roll in a towel or light piece of cloth toward the clew of the sail.

Jiffy reefing got its name because it's fast, but it's hardly elegant. The machinery is simple enough—a variation (as noted earlier) of the Cunningham tackle. When jiffy reefing, a hook secures the sail luff down to the boom, while a tackle pulls the leech down and out. The key to the system is the position of the reefing block that controls the leech: it must be spotted on the boom just a bit farther out than the position of the leech reefing clew when the sail is reefed, so it can exert both an outward and a downward pull. Frequently the line leads forward to a small winch, also mounted on the boom, to get enough tension along the sail foot and leech. The sail remains raised during the maneuver, and the excess area is allowed to bag or is lashed with a light line, according to the whim of the skipper.

Going to windward in heavy weather may be splashy fun for a while, but it soon gets wearisome, especially when you have no choice. Many skippers find it easier on boat and crew to motorsail—head off enough to keep the mainsail filled, and use the engine to drive the boat. This technique keeps the boat steady and on her feet, and if you can allow the bow to fall off the wind enough to get some drive in the main, you may even increase your speed perceptibly.

In heavy seas, reaching is of course the safest and fastest way to sail, but as one heads further and further off the wind, the danger of a runaway jibe becomes greater. Running in heavy weather was discussed earlier, but it cannot hurt to reemphasize that the crew should be well aft in small boats, the mainsail should be vanged to a sturdy deck fitting, and the sheets should be tended all the time.

Eventually, wind and sea may become too much for safe or bearable sailing. In this connection, the modern boat not stripped out for racing is likely to endure much more of a beating than her crew can take. The choices before the skipper will vary according to the wind force and direction, his desired destination, and the seaworthiness of his boat. The simplest thing—and one often adopted by daysailers and small cruisers during squalls—is to lower and tightly furl all sail, secure the boom, lash the tiller and wait for conditions to improve. Called *lying a-hull*, this tactic will serve when there's enough room down to leeward and when waves are not too high and steep.

If the boat will do it, *heaving to* is more comfortable and produces less leeway. With a small amount of sail aft, the sheet is made fast amidships or slightly to port and the tiller is lashed well over to port—not enough to stall, but tied firmly to keep the rudder fittings from unnecessary working. The boat should fall off onto a starboard tack reach, head up until the sail luffs, then fall off and repeat the process. The advantage of heaving to on starboard tack is that your vessel, which is technically under way, will automatically have right of way over all port-tack craft in International Rule areas, and over port-tack vessels not close-hauled Inland. On the other hand, if there is land off to port, you'll be better off on the other tack, as the boat should edge her way slowly first upwind and then to leeward.

Not all sloops will heave to, but nearly all two-masted rigs will, under mizzen or (in the case of schooners) fully reefed mainsail. Unless the seas are very high, a properly hove-to vessel will ride easy and dry, like a gull on water. If your boat doesn't respond to the classical sail-tiller arrangement, experiment with others; some craft do very well with a storm jib and the tiller strapped down to the same side. The aim remains the same—to allow the boat to respond to wind and wave without battling them, and at the same time to keep her from rolling out of control.

Certain vessels which won't heave to happily under any conditions will respond to a sea anchor off the bow or stern. Before investing in one, you can rig a makeshift with your smallest jib, using lines led from the corners to form a sort of triangular parachute: If the boat rides easily and keeps her bow or stern up close to the wind—but not right into it—then an orthodox sea anchor should perform even better.

Your heavy anchor, with chain and a long

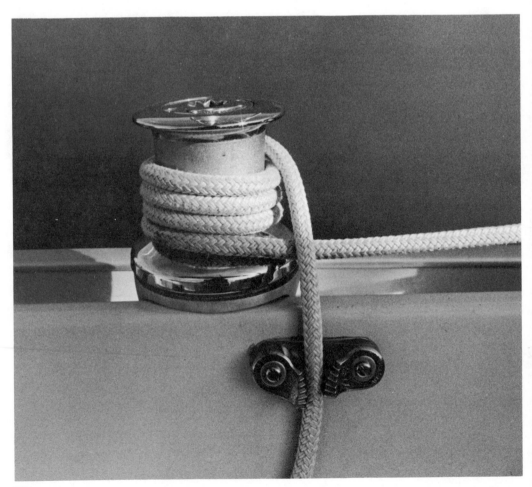

rode, will also make a sizable drag from the bow—with the added advantage that you'll at least have warning before you run ashore, even if the anchor doesn't succeed in taking the bottom.

While one could go on at length about the various precautions possible for different boats in different circumstances, it would require at least a book, and someone has already provided an excellent one. Skippers who regularly sail stormy waters or off inhospitable coastlines will do well to read and consider the information in Richard Henderson's *Sea Sense* (International Marine Publishing Co.,

Camden, Maine: 1972), which covers all aspects of seamanship.

For most of us, however, serious storms are well forecast or of short duration. What we must do is keep the boat afloat and off the shore, and stay with her. It is a tragedy too often repeated that a boat will come through a storm battered but safe, while the crew who abandoned her have not made it. As long as your boat is above water, you are safer and easier to find if you're in her, and the shore is nearly always farther away than it looks.

Part III. Equipment And Maintenance

16. The Trailer Sailer

Given reasonable luck and average winds, the small sailing cruiser ambles along at about 4 knots: sail for 10 hours and you're 40 miles from where you started. Once you've explored your normal sailing grounds exhaustively, you have to use a day or more of valuable vacation time to get to the beginning of new territory—and you have to budget another day (or two if you're conservative) on the way home. But if you can fit your boat on an over-the-highway trailer, you can begin your vacation a hundred—or several hundred—miles from home, explore waters you'd never normally see, and keep the boat in the driveway during the off-season, where you can work on her in the odd hour or two and pay no yard bill.

For all these reasons, trailer boating as a

whole has taken an incredible leap during the last decade or so, and sailors have formed a considerable fraction of the total. Even so, outboard skippers are the real pioneers in this field, and much of the gear (plus most of the skills) were evolved by and for owners of day-cruising speedboats. Much of it will work for the sailboat owner, with a certain amount of adaptation.

The basic parameter for trailer sailing is a boat no more than eight feet wide, that being the maximum width for highway trailering without special permits in most states. With such permits, many states will let you haul a boat up to 10 feet in beam, but beyond that width, towing is a job for the commercial wide-load specialists. Some states also have laws concerning the total length of the rig—boat plus towing vehicle—a combined LOA being 50 feet in many areas. Unless

A good type of sailboat hull for launching from a trailer. Note the guides and roller for the keel.

yours is an abnormally long tow car, you shouldn't have to worry, because the usual length of a large trailerable sailboat seldom exceeds 25 feet.

Unless your trailer yacht is dry-sailed and launched each time with a crane, as some racers are, your boat's hull will have to be shaped so it can be hauled and launched with reasonable ease right off the trailer bed. Early trailerable sailboats had trouble fitting the standard trailers available, but now stock or semicustom trailers are available with beds to fit virtually any boat narrow enough to be trailed. The ideal bottom for a ramp-launching trailer has no projections—even the vestigial keel of a standard cruising centerboarder can hang up when trying to slide it on or off.

If you're buying a trailerable sailboat, try to get a demonstration launch from a vehicle the boat manufacturer recommends; if you're thinking of putting wheels on a boat you already own, consult the builder and/or the designer. Chances are, they have already given a good deal of thought to the matter. If a standard model trailer isn't available to fit your boat, it's usually possible to replace the rollers with properly shaped bunks or bolsters, and these may be as simple as segments of 1x6 or 1x8 timber, padded with carpet scraps. It won't be the easiest kind of launch, but it will work.

There are two kinds of boat trailering, calling for two levels of equipment. First is for

the owner who really wants a cradle on wheels, adequate for supporting the boat at home in the off season and towable—very slowly—to a nearby launching place twice a season. If this arrangement appeals to you, and the local traffic authorities aren't too strict, you can save a good deal of money by buying an undersize or home-made trailer. Most of the safety factors in commercial trailers are designed to cope with wheeling along at turnpike speeds. Damn near anything can limp down the road to the harbor and back twice a year.

If this is what you want, get an underweight standard trailer, and chock it up when the boat is resting on it in the off-season, or buy a rebuilt truck chassis, consisting of frame, wheels, and custom wood-block chocks. This beast is as clumsy as it looks and highly illegal almost everyplace—yet visible nearly everywhere, too. Cost, complete from your friendly junk dealer, will probably be around $200—but be sure to check the unwritten rules in your area about using such a vehicle.

For serious, high-speed trailing, the requirments are, quite properly, much more severe. These demands are in two areas—those legally prescribed and those derived from common sense. Legal requirements vary, and in many states trailer equipment rules are in the process of change, as authorities at last turn official attention to the horde of boat trailers around. For up-to-the-minute information, consult your state police and/or motor vehicle bureau.

Besides beam and total length, regulations commonly deal with total weight load, although state laws vary enormously in this area. The American Boat & Yacht Council, a semiofficial standards-making body, feels that brakes should be an available option (at least) on all wheels of all trailers designed for a gross weight (vehicle and load) of 1,500 pounds or more.

Laws usually require, in addition, lights and license plates. If possible, make sure that the rear lights and license plate on your trailer are removable, so you can take them off before backing the trailer into the water. No matter what manufacturers may say, no lighting system made can survive both highway vibration and repeated immersion.

Trailer brakes come in three common types—*surge, electrical,* and *hydraulic.* The surge brake, activated by the trailer's own momentum, is not under the driver's control, and is illegal in an increasing number of states. Both electrical and hydraulic systems, on the other hand, are accepted everywhere. Your braking system should operate automatically with the towing vehicle's service brakes, and it should continue to operate even if the trailer breaks free of the tow car.

There are also three kinds of towing hitches, the attachments that connect trailer and car. In ascending order of capacity, they are the low-strength *bumper hitch,* which clamps directly to the tower's bumper, and which is not accepted in many states; the *frame hitch,* which bolts to at least two of the tow vehicle's structural members; and the *weight-distributing hitch,* a complicated device that uses leverage on both car and trailer to distribute the load evenly and keep the towing vehicle level with the road. A frame hitch is adequate for gross weights of 3,500 pounds or less; above that the weight-distributing hitch is necessary.

A key point in the hitch is the ball and socket connector between car and trailer. For some reason, the two standard sizes of towing ball are only an eighth of an inch apart in diameter (2″ and 1-7/8″), and they are not interchangeable. Don't expect to be able to eyeball the difference until you've used your trailer a good deal. The smaller ball is for gross loads up to a ton, and the larger is for heavier weights. Towing balls can be forced out of true by wear, so you should carry an extra among your spares. If it gets around that you have a serviceable tow vehicle, you may be asked to pull a trailer for a friend, and thus a towing ball of the other size, whatever it be, is useful too. Like all bolts on your trailer, the one holding the towing ball should be fitted with a lock nut.

The final legal requirement in most states is a pair of safety chains. These consist simply of two chains with S-hooks run from the trailer tongue to the towing hitch, and crossed under the hitch in such a manner that if the ball-and-socket fails, the trailer tongue will be supported off the ground—so it won't drop, dig in and cause the trailer to do a high-speed somersault. The chains should be just long enough to permit a nonbinding turn and should be hooked as shown to prevent their jumping free.

The chains themselves should be welded

Safety chains connecting trailer and towing vehicle should be crossed, as here, under the trailer's tongue.

steel with a breaking test load equivalent to that of the trailer's recommended gross weight. Some trailer sailors use a single length of chain, passed through the eyes on the trailer tongue, but individually attached chains provide an extra safety factor. In no case should the chains be attached to a fastener common with the ball, for obvious reasons.

It is vital that the trailer properly support your boat's hull. Even sturdy fiberglass vessels can be badly wrenched out of shape if they're not braced at critical points, but the difficulty is that hulls are designed to be evenly supported by water, and no roller system can act on them perfectly. For most hulls, the major points to be braced out of water are the forefoot, the keel, the turn of the bilge (especially where interior weights are concentrated) and the transom. Any other spot where a particularly heavy downward force is exerted from inside should be supported from below when the boat is fully seated on the trailer.

In the general category of concentrated weights, you can include retractable keels or centerboards, water tanks, fuel tanks and batteries. If your boat has an inboard engine, this is an absolutely crucial weight concentration, and rollers or bunkers on the trailer should line up right below the engine bed stringers.

On most trailers, the standard rollers and bolsters are adjustable for height and fore-and-aft position, and the winch column and wheel assemblies can be moved along the frame. Given a trailer of adequate length, you should be able to adjust the various elements of the frame and the supports to match your boat. Remember, however, to be very precise when moving any part that has a matching component on the trailer's opposite side: An

TIRE LOAD CAPACITY AT VARIOUS INFLATIONS

Tire Size	Ply Rating	30	35	40	45	50	55	60	65	70	75	80	85	90	95	100
4.80/4.00 x 8	2	380														
4.80/4.00 x 8	4	380	420	450	485	515	545	575	600							
5.70/5.00 x 8	4		575	625	665	710										
5.70/5.00 x 8°	6		575	625	665	710	750	790	830	865	900					
5.70/5.00 x 8°	8		575	625	665	710	750	790	830	865	900	930	965	1000	1030	
6.90/6.00 x 9	4			785	850											
6.90/6.00 x 9	6			785	850	915	970	1030	1080							
6.90/6.00 x 9	8			785	850	915	970	1030	1080	1125	1175	1225	1270			
6.90/6.00 x 9°	10			785	850	915	970	1030	1080	1125	1175	1225	1270	1320	1365	1410 1450
20 x 8.00-10	4	825	900													
20 x 8.00-10	6	825	900	965	1030	1100										
20 x 8.00-10	8	825	900	965	1030	1100	1155	1210	1270	1325						
20 x 8.00-10	10	825	900	965	1030	1100	1155	1210	1270	1325	1370	1420	1475			
4.80/4.00 x 12	4	545	550	595	635	680	715	755	790							
5.30/4.50 x 12	4	640	700	760	810	865	915									
5.30/4.50 x 12	6	640	700	760	810	865	915	960	1005	1045	1090	1135				
6.00 x 12	4	855	935	1010												
6.00 x 12	6	855	935	1010	1090	1160	1230	1290								

inch or so of fore-and-aft maladjustment between the wheels can cause a serious riding problem for the whole rig.

A trailer's tires and wheels undergo far more strain than do the ones on your car. Not only are a trailer's wheels subject to immersion (often in salt or heavily polluted water), but they are smaller and must therefore turn at far higher speeds. Tire pressures for various standard loads are usually given in a decal on the trailer itself, and are also noted in the accompanying chart. As you can see, they are considerably higher than the pressures in ordinary car tires. You should carry a pressure gauge and check the air frequently; if you err, it should be on the side of higher pressure, not lower: Too little air in small, high-speed tires causes them to heat up faster and fail sooner.

Under way on the highway, a trailed boat is subject to a type of rapid motion that it will never encounter on the water. Not only should every unattached piece of gear in the trailer be firmly secured, but also the boat itself should be properly lashed in place. The first point of attachment is forward, at the winch. For people who plan to do their own launching and recovery, the trailer's winch is an especially important piece of equipment, and deserves a few words to itself.

Usually an extra-cost item, the winch should have an antireverse gear, so the boat cannot excape, and should be equipped with wire cable, not rope, except in the case of very light daysailers. For cruising vessels, geared winches and electrical winches running off the car battery are available. The winch drum should be, if possible, approximately on a line with the towing eye (if any) on your boat's bow. If there's no such stem eye, the angle of pull from deck to winch should be slightly downward. Do not expect the winch cable to hold the bow on the trailer unaided. An extra wire cable, preferably with its own turnbuckle, should connect the boat's stem to the winch pillar. In addition, there should be a nonstretch webbing strap with a tensioning buckle across the after part of the boat, and on larger boats a pair of spring lines or straps from the bow aft to the trailer frame at the wheels. Webbing straps are less likely than lines to mar the boat's finish, but it doesn't hurt to carry some 6-inch squares of carpeting to place between any tie-down and the boat.

Useful extras include the following: spare trailer wheel; bearing grease; complete set of wheel bearings; trailer light bulbs (they don't burn out, they die from vibration); a jack, unless your car jack will work on the lower frame of a trailer; a set of long-handle wrenches for tightening the various frame bolts; outside mirrors for your car; flares, trouble flag and trouble light; and for very heavy trailer loads, booster brakes and heavy-duty shock absorbers for the tow vehicle.

In order to tow successfully, you must first balance the load on the trailer. The idea is to get a calculated fraction of the gross weight (trailer *and* load, remember) on the trailer tongue. That fraction should be between 5 and 7 percent of the gross, but not much over 100 pounds for an ordinary passenger car; working backward, that means that most standard sedans are suited to loads of 2,000 pounds or less.

To find the tongue weight, put a set of bathroom scales on a couple of cinder blocks and ease the trailer tongue down on this improvised weighing platform. If the tongue weight is more than you can easily manage (yet within the 5 to 7 percent), consider adding a dolly wheel to the tongue as a safety factor.

When tongue weight is much more than the recommended maximum, your car will have too much load behind and will be hard to handle at road speeds. If the tongue weight is too low, the trailer will have a tendency to fishtail.

Before setting out, check the weights in the trailer to make sure they're firmly chocked or

Combination of bow pulpit and metal brackets in mast base fitting and flagpole socket give excellent traveling support.

lashed in place. People have a bad habit of tossing things into boats and forgetting them, and a trailer-mounted boat is usually too high to see into from the ground. Check also that the trailer's frame bolts are tight and that the lights and brakes work. These connections between car and trailer are always tricky and subject to failure.

The mast should be lashed down firmly, with the rigging bundled and tied off so it can't escape. Consider getting or making padded supports for the spar at bow, midships and stern, and possibly wrapping at least the masthead and winch area to keep dust and grit out. If the mast extends aft of the transom, tie a red flag to the end.

Under way, it will often require an effort to remember that you've got a boat tailing along behind, especially once you're moving at full speed. Start slowly, in low gear, and take the

car easily up through the speeds to high. Think twice about passing other vehicles, but if you decide to do it, don't dither. Make certain your entire trailed load is past before cutting back into the right-hand lane. Remain alert to any unusual sounds or handling factors, and if you have any doubts at all, pull over and see.

You should, in fact, pull off the road every hour or so to check the rig: hot wheel bearings, slackening tiedowns, lights, tire pressure, car engine temperature.

Before you attempt a launching, you should spend a couple of hours some Sunday afternoon in the local supermarket parking lot, learning how to back the rig properly. It's a lot easier than docking, but it does take practice. Many people find that steering in reverse is easier if they keep their hands on the bottom of the wheel, and you should make the most use of your side mirrors, rather than relying on peering out the door. If your rig is exceptionally unwieldy, you may want to invest in a front bumper hitch, which will make close quarters maneuvering much simpler.

When launching, try to avoid getting the

trailer hubs in the water—though this is often impossible. If you can't help dunking them, at least let them cool off first—if you don't, the heat will simply suck the bearing full of water. One way to pass the time while waiting for the wheels to cool is by stepping the mast in the parking lot—where it's usually easier than afloat or on the ramp anyway. Before you begin, park the car in a place where there's a clear route to the ramp, with no overhanging electrical wires in the way. Most launching ramps were laid out for the use of small outboard skiffs, not sailboats, and several people have been killed when their metal masts hit improperly insulated wires.

Sailboat masts are usually stepped from astern forward. In smaller boats, one person guides the foot of the spar into the step, while the other raises the mast. In boats over 16 feet

Raising a hinged mast from aft forward. One crewmember must get the mast partway up before the other can begin to exert an effective pull with the forestay. For safety and a better grip, a pair of gloves would be a big help.

When the mast hinges from forward aft, as on this Ericson 25, one can use the multi-part mainsheet to raise the spar. Note how guy wires are rigged from the boom to the chainplates, with the upper shrouds tied into the system.

or so, the spar is usually hinged at the foot, with a removable pin connecting the mast foot and the tabernacle on deck. The mast may, in some cases, swing up and aft when being raised: that is, the spar lies flat over the foredeck when first made fast to its hinge; the upper shrouds are attached on either side, and the forestay, and then the boom is attached to the gooseneck and raised to a vertical position, held there by the topping lift and temporary guys to the deck on either side. To raise the spar, you simply employ the four or five-part advantage of the mainsheet.

Masts that raise forward from a position over the stern are simpler to get up, but take more human effort as a rule. Attach the upper shrouds and the backstay, and tie a line to the forestay (don't try to grasp the wire). As one person stands in the cockpit and raises the spar, the bow hand pulls on the forestay extension. If the boat is very small and light, without floorboards, the mast lifter will do better not to get into the boat at all.

In the process of launching or recovery, be sure that the rudder and the centerboard or lifting keel are fully raised. When the boat is on the trailer, however, the keel pennant should be eased so the weight rests on a cross-member of the trailer. Never turn the car engine off during launch or recovery, and if you have an automatic transmission, leave it in *low* with the brake set while you maneuver the boat on or off the trailer. Professional boating people like to shoot the boat off the trailer by backing down the ramp and then, as the stern begins to lift, braking sharply. This works well, but a second person must be standing ashore with a line made fast to the boat's bow, and the shock can pull him or her right into the water.

When the boat is on her trailer for any length of time, get the weight off the tires and springs. Block up the four corners of the trailer frame and the tongue with cinder blocks, shimmed up to level with 1x8 planks.

128

Once the trailer frame is jacked up, check that the rollers are still supporting the boat, as the frame can twist out of its normal shape in the jacking process. Wheels should be off the ground enough to spin free, and you should use this as a time to check the wheel bearings and repack them if necessary.

None of this is as complicated as it may seem on paper—it soon becomes second nature, like releasing the mainsheet before making sail. After all, outboarders have been doing most of these things for years.

17. Electrics

With each passing year, more and more electrical and electronic equipment is routinely found aboard even the smallest sailing vessels, and larger cruisers carry electronics of really staggering complexity. This is not a book on electricity aboard your boat (a couple of titles are suggested in the Bibliography), but a few things should be said about the selection and use of this kind of equipment for small daysailers and cruisers.

What's lacking in the average sailboat—as compared to a house or even a powerboat of equal size—is an adequate generating source. Coupled with this, in most cases, is an equivalent lack of electrical storage capacity; while a house hardly needs to store electricity, a boat cut off from a constantly operating generator does need to be able to carry reserve capacity along with it. In a powerboat, the more or less constantly operating engine meets the boat's running demands, while storage batteries and/or a generator provide power when the main engines aren't running.

Most modern powerboats with accommodation also have shore-power—a separate 110-volt system which is activated by plugging into a socket at dockside. The ship's 12 (or more)-volt system is used when away from shore, but at least the engines and generator are unnecessary when tied up at a marina.

shore, but at least the engines and generator are unnecessary when tied up at a marina. The same two-system electrical rig is now seen on increasing numbers of larger sailing cruisers with advanced electrical requirements, but for the most part, it's a needless complexity, not to mention an extra cost.

There are lots of old salts around who decry the presence of electrical gadgets aboard, and beyond a certain level of equipment it's quite possible to agree with them. But by and large electricity in moderation is a good friend to the sailor, simplifying his life and making his boating safer.

Let's look at the electrical requirements which might be common aboard three different kinds of boats, and then try to establish what sort of electrical system could be devised to meet them. It's helpful, when buying a new boat, to consider electrical and electronic needs right from the start, so as to be able to do the most work with the least complexity of gear. Especially batteries: self-powered electrical devices can use more than half a dozen sizes of portable battery, which means that in order to be able to rely on them, one might have to carry half a dozen sizes of spares.

By shopping around for your various flashlights and other equipment, you should be able to keep the range of battery sizes for self-powered gear down to a minimum. Even so, you'll probably have to have a batch of C and D cells, and probably a couple of 9-volt transistor batteries, too. You should have enough spare batteries aboard, in a sealed container, to replace all the cells in the largest instrument or device using each size battery. And you may want to invest a few more bucks in getting rechargeable heavy duty batteries and a home battery charger—after a season afloat, the batteries may never be as good as new, but they will serve when topped up for household use.

As for the boat's main battery, you will want the 12 volt storage unit with the largest ampere-hour capacity your boat's battery stowage compartment can accommodate. If you use the boat only occasionally and don't have a charger or engine generator, then consider using your car battery.

The daysailer which gets an occasional run after dark is probably the minimum user of power—above none at all, that is. She should carry running lights for operation in both power and sail modes, an anchor light, a flashlight, and a portable radio receiver for weather forecasts (over and above its normal uses). My choice for this boat's running and anchor lights would be the clamp-on type, powered by D cells. They can be taken home and kept dry when not in use, and their light, while not great, is probably adequate to the occasion.

The ship's flashlight should be somewhat more advanced, however, as it will have to serve both for groping under the foredeck and as a warning light—when shone on the sails, it will attract large boats' attention far quicker than will the running lights. A waterproof three or four-cell light is a minimum. As for a radio, I would be inclined to splurge and buy a portable which can receive both the commercial and the VHF-FM band providing continuous weather forecasts from the National Oceanographic and Atmospheric Administration. These broadcasts are on either 162.4 or 162.55 MHz, depending on your location, and thus are slightly higher frequency than the standard commercial FM stations. Some FM radios have this band, some don't, but if you ask for a set which will get the marine FM weather band, the clerk should know what you're talking about.

The pocket cruiser that often goes under the nickname of *overnighter* or *weekender* is the next size up. The builder may supply a running light installation in the standard price, but if he doesn't, portable lights should serve well enough for this boat, too. A

129

portable anchor light is another good investment—even if this kind of boat has a storage battery, you don't want to impose on it with an all-night light of fairly high intensity.

The flashlight aboard this size vessel should be more in the nature of a portable spotlight, with a six volt lantern cell or half a dozen D cells as power. And it should be waterproof: no light aboard a boat will work long if moisture can get into it. You should carry a life ring or horseshoe buoy for man-overboard situations, and to it should be attached a self-activating man-overboard light. This is usually a flashing or flickering white light which hangs upside down alongside the life ring. When tossed over the side with the ring, it floats right side up, which activates the interior gravity switch, turning it on.

Your boat will probably have one or more cabin lights, too. Lights in a cabin don't have to be extensive—at the least, a single one will serve; the maximum installation would call for one low-power bulb at the head of each berth, for reading, another at the galley and possibly another in the head compartment, if it's separate from other cabins. Your steering compass should be lit, with a red bulb, using its own lantern cell or hooked into the boat's 12 volt system, and of course you will want a portable radio receiver aboard, too.

The small cruising boat, in which serious voyaging can be accomplished in a reasonably civilized manner, will have a built-in electrical system. It should be fully fused, with separate circuits for running and anchor lights and for the ship's own system. A couple of spare circuits are nice to have as well, for future equipment. Your boat's running lights will almost certainly be built in, and you may have—if the boat has been built by a careful manufacturer—separate circuits for the sailing lights and the additional steaming light, which shows your boat is under power. You may also have a masthead anchor light, which can be very effective but which still is a con-

siderable drain on the system when used, as it's likely to be used, for several nights running during a cruise, without much chance to top off during the day.

In addition to a man-overboard light, if you sail frequently at night, you should have individual life preserver lights for the crew on deck. Your portable spot should be as big and powerful as you can find, and you should also have a spare, waterproof flashlight for ordinary work. Your boat may come equipped, either as standard or more likely as an extra-cost option, with work lights mounted under the spreaders or on the forward side of the mast. Except for ocean racers which need the light for after-dark sail changing, I think spreader lights are far more trouble than they're worth. They seldom seem to work in any case, which is not surprising: there are usually two connectors for each wire (one at the spreader, one at the base of the mast), and the whole installation is vulnerable to every flap of a genoa. Too, when suddenly turned on, the light from above impartially blinds everyone on deck.

If, however, yours is one of those rare small cruisers with a surface suited to chartwork down below, be sure to get a good chart light. This can be the nearest cabin light with the bulb painted red, but far better is to install a focusing light on a gooseneck, with its bulb also reddened (nail polish works fine) to preserve the navigator's night vision. If you don't have a chart installation, then you should have a spare flashlight with a red lens for this kind of work.

I've said nothing about navigational gear so far, unless one counts chart table and compass illumination. The truth is, though this kind of comment does not make one popular in the marine equipment business, very little electronic gear is useful, let alone necessary, aboard the small auxiliary. Hand-operated charting equipment, a good compass, and perhaps—very perhaps—a leadline for checking depths in anchorages.

A lot is available, though. Perhaps the first electronic device most skippers fall for is a depth sounder. Presumably one uses it in navigation by matching a line of soundings on the chart with the periodic depth indications on the sounder, but this is seldom attempted. There are certain circumstances in which it might be regularly useful, however, and I participated in one of them not too long ago when I took a shallow-draft ketch down into the shoal waters of Long Island's Great South Bay. There are parts of that body of water where one can stand waist deep a couple of miles from the nearest shore, and I had the sounder on more or less continually, to confirm that there was still a foot or so under the keel.

If you sail in shoal waters where the shoaling is gradual, a depth sounder will provide a good deal of reassurance and may help keep you off the ground. It will also tell you of very obvious and gross changes in water depth which can usually be seen on the chart—river canyons and major bars which are not dangers to navigation and hence not buoyed. Other than that, it remains largely a toy, albeit a fascinating one.

For my money—and that's how I spent it—the depth sounder is best mounted inside a fiberglass hull, with its transducer head up against the boat's bottom. That means you can't wipe the transducer off the hull when hauling the boat, and it doesn't get fouled with grass and barnacles. Properly installed, the instrument loses some 15 to 50 percent of its sensitivity, which means it won't probe as deep—it still reads correctly. At least one firm offers a kit with its instrument: a fitted and capped plastic tube, which contains the transducer and is cut to fit the inside curve of the hull; plus epoxy putty to make a watertight bond; plus a small bottle of castor oil, of all things, to fill the tube. It works fine.

Next most popular perhaps is the portable

radio direction finder. If you don't ask too much of one of these things, you can get very general bearings on commercial radio stations and on marine radio beacons. Not precise enough for a good fix, but enough to tell you that a given place is now more or less abeam. Should you decide to spring for one of these, get a set with as many bands as possible, so you can also receive the VHF-FM marine weather and the ordinary marine MF channels in the 2-3 MHz band.

A speedometer is something that can be very useful indeed aboard a sailboat, even if its absolute readings are quite wrong, as they often are. It will be a definite asset in sail trim exercises, indicating relative gains and losses of speed as the sheets are handled and the sails' shapes changed. It need not be electronic at all—there are several styles which draw power from the little in-the-water spinner that registers how fast you're going.

And a radio transmitter. For most skippers, that now means a VHF-FM set, as medium-frequency licenses are no longer being granted, and the citizens' band sets are really not adequate for the real purpose of two-way radio, distress calls. Prices of VHF-FM transceivers have gone down in recent years (yes, *down*) as the manufacturers of them have managed to sell enough to institute production-line savings in assembly costs. They are still nothing like cheap, and you would do well to check, before buying one, that there are adequate Coast Guard radio installations in your boating area so you'll be heard on the air.

Range for a VHF-FM set is approximately line-of-sight—less than 6 miles for a deck-mounted antenna, perhaps 20 or 25 from your 30-foot masthead to the 150-foot antenna at the Coast Guard station. In a few years there should be overlapping Coast Guard monitoring facilities all over the country's coastal and inland waters. At this writing, however, there are still sizable areas where your chances of

131

being heard are very slender.

As for the many other more esoteric electronic navigational devices—relative wind indicators, automatic direction finders, Loran and the like—I think you are far better off without them until you own a boat in the 40-foot class and find yourself entered in the Bermuda, Mackinac or TransPac.

Power supply for the equipment you *do* have must be either from self-contained batteries or the ship's storage battery. My own feeling is that a piece of gear should, if possible, be self-contained—both so it will work when the main system fails and so that if it goes, it won't take anything else with it. Depth sounders, RDFs and speedometers are all available with their own batteries. If your circumstances allow it, I would recommend that a VHF-FM set have its own battery—a standard 12-volt storage job—separate from the boat's own engine battery, but capable of being topped up by the engine's generator or alternator.

Other useful accessories are a battery condition indicator, which is a small, inexpensive instrument that shows what its name indicates, extra fuses, an ammeter on your engine dashboard, and if you carry two batteries, a two-position safety switch, which will allow you to use both batteries in starting the engine, or either one.

18. Sailboat Maintenance

A reasonably observant person needs to own a modern boat for about a month to appreciate how much work is still involved in the upkeep of a fiberglass hull with Dacron and nylon sails and stainless steel rigging. About the only consolation is the fact that maintenance today is far less complex and demanding than it used to be—just as well, now that so few skippers can afford to farm the work out.

And this leads to an important point which must be considered right at the start. If you keep your boat in a yard or marina in the off season, you should come to an agreement with the management about exactly what kind of work you're permitted to do on your boat, and what (if any) outside experts you may import. The economics of boatyards often require that nearly all work be handled by resident personnel—but this can become fantastically expensive at double-digit hourly rates. By looking around at less pretentious yards, you can usually find one where the owner couldn't care less what you do to your boat. If you're lucky, you may even find a small establishment where the proprietor specializes in one area of boat repair, and it's something (like engine maintenance) which you don't or can't handle yourself.

For the purposes of this chapter, we'll assume that you want to handle most of the nontechnical work yourself, and that the yard will let you. Your tool requirements are not great —the table in Chapter 19 suggests what you'll need for the small daysailer or cruiser—and the work itself is elementary for the most part, especially if you plan ahead and don't let it pile up.

Hulls are of course common to all boats, and the hull work for sailboats is not so different from that on powercraft. In this category, as in the ones which follow, I propose to take the common maintenance chores for a given segment of the boat through a sailing year. Your haul-out and storage season may be six months or it may be a week and a half, but the jobs involved tend to be much the same. About the only major maintenance differences between parts of the country are concerned with the presence or absence of freezing temperatures for part of the year.

Hulls and interiors

When your off-season work on the boat comes to an end, you can begin to see launching day in the distance. As with a train coming right at you, for a long time there seems to be no increase in nearness, and then suddenly it's on top of you.

With your winter's repairs and installations done, your first job is to clean the stripped-out interior—something which can nearly always be better done ashore than afloat. The whole inside of the hull should be scrubbed with hot water (How will you heat it? How about a vacuum jug?) and a cleaner-detergent such as Lysol. Start with the overhead and work down. When you come across little piles of shavings or unidentifiable dirt, don't soak it—vacuum it up first.

You'll wind up with a dreadful bilge. Don't pump it out—you'll probably just choke up the pump—unless yours is a diaphragm-type bilge pump. Scrub the empty bilge with disinfectant and perhaps a not-too-abrasive cleaner. This can be hell on sponges, especially if the inner hull is unfinished fiberglass, which simply rips sponges to tiny, adhesive shreds. Use a stiff-bristle brush or an extra-thick abrasive cloth in tough spots.

When you're through, dry the bilge out to the last drop with a sponge. Wait an hour or two, and dry it out again. Now you can replace those instruments and furniture removed before haulout. Before launching, all through-hull plumbing must be checked to make sure it's closed in the *off* position.

Check and dewinterize the plumbing. In my cruising catboat, the entire plumbing system consisted of a portable toilet, a sink pump, a portable five -gallon water tank, and a length of plastic hose. Everything but the sink pump went home with me. Most cruising boats are not so elemental: You will have to drain the antifreeze from the pumps and water lines, and if your water tasted odd toward the end of last season, open the water tanks and scrub the interiors, or as much of them as you can reach. A small dose of one of the water-purifying agents available in most marinas will also help prevent your coffee from tasting as if it had been brewed in an old shoe.

When you're finished inside, lock the boat up and move on deck. Check the outside ends of all through-hull fittings, especially the steering gear. Make sure there is no play in the rudder fittings and that the pintles still fit closely but not tightly in the gudgeons.

If the boat has been covered, now is the time to remove the canvas, wash and if necessary patch it, and stow it away for the summer. Disassemble your winter cover frame, being careful to mark each piece, and put it away, too. If the frame is light wood, one or more pieces may have to be replaced. A winter frame can be quite simple, constructed of inexpensive fir or pine 1x3; basically, it consists of three or more uprights along the boat's centerline, the highest in the middle. Atop this runs the frame backbone, which can be planking of convenient length to carry in or atop your car, with bolted overlap sections to make it one continuous piece slightly longer than the boat.

Ribs run down from the backbone at intervals of four or five feet, extending well over the gunwales or lifeline stanchions (to which they can be lashed). The most important thing to remember is that the frame should be padded with carpeting at every sharp corner, including the ends of the ribs, to avoid tearing the cover. If the boat is quite beamy, run a couple of parallels to the backbone. The idea is to avoid any potential pockets which may collect snow or rain.

With the cover off, you can clean and wax the deck and cabin top and sides. Most fiberglass boats have large patches of nonskid pattern molded into the deck. About the only way to clean this diamond-shaped dirtcatcher is with a stiff-bristled brush and a lot of muscle. If your boat has a substantial area of deck, get a brush with a long handle. In any case, you may also want a pair of those rubber knee-pads sold in gardening shops.

When cleaning plexiglass or other plastic portholes, be sure not to use an abrasive compound. Clean them with a chamois and soapy water that hasn't been used for anything else. Plastic ports scratch easily and permanently, and it's all too easy to ruin them in short order.

Clean and wax all the fittings on deck and cabin, and then move down to do the wood trim. Most boats today are finished off with untreated teak, which is something of a misnomer, because it requires fairly constant attention in order to remain looking untreated. One good prescription for this wood is to use a brand-name teak cleaner or a highly abrasive powder, following the directions carefully. When this is done, go over the wood again with bronze wool. (Never use steel wool on a boat—it leaves tiny bits of itself in corners, something you notice later by the rust streaks.) You should now have a gorgeous white or light pinky-brown finish. Don't leave it that way, but apply a coat or two of teak sealer, a specialized oil that darkenes the wood just a bit, but preserves it as well. Don't splatter the oil, which is nearly invisible but which, on nonporous surfaces, attracts dirt like flypaper.

Next the hull above the waterline. Scrub it with any good, nonabrasive cleaner (you may have to use a little abrasive on especially tough stains, like the ones down the sides which can build up where water drains off the deck), doing a patch at a time and hosing off while it's still wet. Follow up with a substantial waxing, using any of the boat or car waxes on the market. The object is not necessarily to achieve a high shine (let your conscience be

A hull envelope, like the one around this Northwest 21, can keep marine growth at bay with the aid of a little chemical.

your guide) but to protect the boat's skin from fading and becoming lifeless.

Launch time is rapidly approaching, and now is the point to come to grips with the bottom. If you're lucky enough to have a lot of help, you can put one or two of them to sanding and filling the bottom while the others are waxing the topsides. A boat's bottom should be as smooth and obstruction-free as you can get it, which often means not only sanding off the scabby paint of yesteryear but also filling in with epoxy putty any scratches and gouges picked up last season.

When the bottom is prepared, you can apply the bottom paint formula of your choice. None of them is perfect, but how incredibly awful the boat's underbody would be without them. Be thankful at least that you don't have to fall back on the traditional antifouling compound of the Persian Gulf—shark fat and lime, applied with the hand. Since you are paying a small fortune for whatever you're using, be sure to follow the maker's directions carefully. Two coats are best on new work, but you can probably get away with one coat thereafter.

If yours is a centerboard boat, you will have to work out some way of painting the inside of the board trunk. With the board removed, you can make shift to do it with a swab of fairly hairy carpeting on the end of a pole. Or you can leave the board in, seal the trunk beneath, and fill it with antifouling from the top. Wait 15 minutes or so, and then drain off the excess paint back into the bucket, to be used on the hull.

You're almost ready to go. The last piece of paintwork before the boat is lifted free of her cradle is whatever touch-up the boot-topping may require. Many owners find it distinctly unsettling to be on hand when their craft is lifted—often by a superannuated crane which scarcely seems man enough for the job. Someone must be available, however, for the final chore—a quick sanding and painting of the spots on the boat's bottom that were unreachable while she sat on the cradle. Unless you can do it yourself, be sure to leave a small amount of antifouling in a sealed jar, plus a paintbrush, where the crane workers will be certain to find it. Otherwise you'll either have patchy barnacles at four points on the bottom or a bill for a can of antifouling and a brush.

As soon as the boat is in the water, and before the crane operator removes the slings, check down below for leaks. Even fiberglass boats leak, and any boat will leak if someone has forgotten to close a through hull fitting. Should you have an untraceable leak, however minute, be certain your pump works before allowing the crane operator to remove himself.

During the season, you should hose off the decks and wipe off the metal fittings after each sail, if possible. In boating areas affected by airborne grime and grit, you'll probably have to rewax the hull and rebleach the teak about once a month or even more. In extremely smoggy areas, you may find it works better to invest in fabric covers for those nonplastic above deck parts that suffer badly—coamings, tillers, winches. Depending on the rapidity with which the marine creatures get used to your brand of bottom paint, you'll also have to scrub or wipe off that part of the hull, too. It's best to get after the boat's underbody as soon as visible signs of scum appear, while they can still be wiped off with a sponge.

Down below, air out the accommodations frequently. In fact, whenever you're aboard on a sunny afternoon, make a point of opening all the hatches and ventilators. Galley and head compartments should be cleaned once every couple of weeks, or after any prolonged use (such as a weekend cruise). Unlike most such installations ashore, a boat's galley and head are horribly cramped, and you may need special tools—sponges on handles, for instance—to get at the corners. However you do it, make certain that the corners do get clean, or you'll regret it.

The portable toilet should be emptied, disinfected, scrubbed, hosed out, and allowed to dry in the sun after each cruise. Much the same procedure is recommended for the icebox, whether it be permanently installed or portable. In either case, leave the lid or door open between voyages.

Water tanks, of whatever material, should be emptied frequently. It's all very well to hoard water while sailing, but as you approach home, encourage everyone to use it up. Then pump out the residue and leave the tank empty till just before you shove off.

At haulout time, strip the boat bare. This is usually easier to do at dockside before she's pulled. Everything comes out—cushions and mattresses, every piece of gear, every block every instrument that can be taken ashore.

With the boat in the slings, the first chore is scrubbing the bottom. Pray for a pleasant day, because this is a wet, smelly job at best. Use a hard-bristled brush on a pole and do a thorough job, hosing off each bit of area while it's still wet. When the boat is placed in her cradle, scrub the part the slings hid, then check that she is chocked up and supported properly—that there is shoring under her inboard engine, and that the hull supports are adequately padded.

Next, scrub and vacuum the interior, with special emphasis on the galley and head. If you have a standard marine toilet, it won't hurt to unbolt and remove it from the boat for a cleaning of those corners of the head compartment—and the head—you couldn't possibly get at while the toilet was *in situ*. Before the cover goes on, give one last treatment to the teak, one last coat of varnish to the mahogany (if any), and a scrub-and-wax to the hull.

Be sure that any winter work which will be impeded by the presence of cover and frame is done now. Will you need water during the

work? Some yards turn off the outside water in winter. If you're planning a major installation, plan also on a major interior cleanup after the work is done. Winterize the boat's plumbing, or instruct the yard to do it (advisable if you have pressure water), well in advance of any freeze. No matter how well you drain the tanks and lines, there will usually be enough water someplace to freeze and pop a tube.

Last step is the frame and cover, which should be secured in such a way that fresh air can get at the boat, but the cover won't fly off. You'll probably want to lock the boat up, but do leave as many vents in and open as you've got. Openings in the cover at bow and stern should provide both air access and a way for you to get aboard. Use good line for tiedowns, and pad them wherever they chafe against the hull.

Spars, sails and rigging

Just before the season, you should unbag and look over the sails to make absolutely sure there is nothing that remains undone. If you have any sense of decency, you will have taken repair work around to your sailmaker in the fall, and all that remains should be trivia, such as renewing the luff telltales on the headsails. Take this opportunity to check the removable sail hardware, so that everything's to hand when you get down to the boat. The luff snaps should work smoothly, but if they don't, a tiny dab of oil can be applied to the pistons.

Now is the time to recheck the battens. If yours are wood, they should have been flattened under a weight over the winter. Warped wood battens can be straightened quickly enough by pouring a kettle of boiling water over them, and then laying them flat under a dead car battery or something equally heavy. Fiberglass battens don't warp, but be sure that the ends are smooth and rounded—padded with rubber is best—so they don't rip the batten pockets.

Before the mast is stepped, you must check the standing rigging, paying extra attention to the masthead, since you won't normally be seeing it again for the rest of the season—unless it falls down on your head. Shackles attaching stays and shrouds to the mast cap should be of the pin rather than the screw type, but if you use the latter, turn them so the eye of the screw is upward, and then wire it closed. Tape the wiring and any other sharp protrusion. If you have lights on the mast—a 20-point or a built-in anchor light—hook them into an auto battery to see that they work.

Rust at the terminals of standing rigging should be a warning to you—detach the piece and take it to a sailmaker who specializes in rigging, and replace it if he so recommends. Replacement is also indicated if *even one* strand of a wire is broken. Likewise, check the turnbuckles and toggles for hairline cracks, using an ordinary magnifying glass. You should carry in your ditty bag a spare for each size of turnbuckle, as well as an emergency wire span and a pair of bulldog clips, in case a wire snaps.

Checking the running rigging means special attention to wire-rope splices, if any. The most common fault is individual wire strands ambushed among the rope, ready to rip your hands or your sails. Tape the splice if necessary, after cutting back the offending strand. Any signs of unusual chafe should suggest both replacement of the worn line and investigation into why the rubbing occurred in the first place.

Sheet and halyard blocks should be both clean and easy running. All the detachable blocks will have spent the off season in a sealed plastic bag, after having been thoroughly washed in fresh water and oiled. Winches can be disassembled, cleaned, and oiled or packed with grease, according to their requirements. For cleaning small parts, kerosene and a stiff-bristled toothbrush are about as effective as anything.

During the season, care of artificial fabric sails is no great problem. They can be stowed wet if necessary, but try to avoid jamming them when damp into mildew-producing lockers if you have the opportunity to hoist them flying free for an hour or so after you finish sailing. Even 15 minutes in a decent breeze will shake most of the moisture off them, and don't forget the sailbags too. Mildew, if it does form, won't harm the sails but it makes an unpleasant stain that's hard to remove.

Keep note of any chafe or breaks in the stitching—on Dacron sails especially, the thread does not sink into the cloth, but "stands proud," and is thus vulnerable to wear. The places to watch in jibs are where the sails hit the spreaders when luffing (your spreaders are, of course, properly taped —aren't they?), mainsails where they rub the aft lower shrouds and around the batten pockets.

Carry adhesive sail repair tape, sailmakers' needles and Dacron thread for temporary repairs under way. Apply the tape generously, then sew it to the sail. Once home, take the sail in for professional help right away. It's amazing how even substantial tears can be repaired if you lower the sail and don't stretch or rip it further.

If you feel that your sails don't set right, try to arrange for the sailmaker to come out with you and see for himself. Failing this, use your camera to photograph the sails when they're setting improperly. Shoot from below upward, as this will accentuate the problem; if the sail's curve doesn't seem right, put long strips of contrasting color tape on the sail and then take your photos. Each picture should be accompanied by a note giving the boat's heading, approximate speed and the wind strength.

No sail cover is required for this roller-furling genoa: The dark colored cloth strip along leech and foot will completely cover the Dacron sail when it's rolled up, keeping sun off.

Nearly all cruising skippers and a lot of daysailers stow their mainsail on the boom. Invest in a sail cover—it's more than worth the expense. Never furl the sail with wood battens still in it—that's a certain way to wind up with warped, if not broken, battens. The cover, by the way, is as much to protect your sail against sunlight as against grit and dirt. It should not fit too tightly underneath, so air can get in, but try to get the collar around the mast as tight as you can—shock cord is probably the best way to achieve a good grip.

To prolong the life of jib and spinnaker sheets, remove and stow them between voyages. Sunlight affects them, too, and airborne grit can work its way into the fibers and accelerate wear. Jib sheets that lie along the deck just inside the gunwales will get not

only what dirt lands on them, but also whatever runoff is washed along them during a shower. The main sheet, which is a troublesome thing to remove each time you sail, should at least be hung in a coil from the underside of the boom.

Halyards cannot normally be hidden, so they have to sit out in the open air and take it. Since your main halyard is exposed anyway, use it to help support the main boom, by hooking it to the topping lift fitting and putting strain on it, rather than on the lift, which is usually a smaller line. A short wire span connected to the backstay is the best way of all to take the load off the lift. If you have a long main boom, buy or make a boom strap—a wide length of canvas with a ring sewn into each end. It will act as a sling to support the center of the boom when you're not sailing, and will serve to spread the load of the boom vang if your mainsail has slides or slugs, so the strap can fit under the foot and over the boom.

When removed from the stay, jibs should

138

be flaked down in easy rolls before being bagged—the idea is to avoid tight, flat folds which may create permanent creases. There's no complete agreement on which end of a jib should protrude from the bag. My personal feeling is that you should have access to the entire luff, tack first, so you can hank on the sail without unbagging it. I prefer to hank on from tack to head, but other sailors like it just the opposite. About the only thing all agree on is that your method should be consistent. And it doesn't hurt to label the tack with india ink or permanent marker.

Most roller furling jibs today come with a wide strip of heavy fabric sewn along the leech and the foot, so that when the sail is rolled up, this protective edging forms a light- and dirt-resistant covering. You should have your sailmaker attach this edging if you have a roller furling jib without it. Don't invest in a jib cover—like a long, narrow mainsail cover, raised on the spinnaker halyard. It will flutter itself to pieces in a fairly short time.

At season's end, sails should be removed from the boat and spread out on a clean, flat surface so you can check them for any signs of wear. Check all three sides, and the stitching of snaps, slides or slugs, as well as luff and foot ropes that run in grooves. If there's nothing wrong, wash the sail in warm water and a detergent, dry it thoroughly, fold it gently and bag it. I usually hang the bag from the basement ceiling, to promote the circulation of air around the sail and to foil field mice who may be looking for a nest.

Repairs and serious cleaning jobs should go to your sailmaker as soon after you decommission as possible. You may get a break on the price of work by giving him the sail before Christmas, and you'll certainly get his best attention. Now is also the time to place orders for whatever other canvas you've talked yourself into for the following season.

Standing rigging should be cleaned and lightly oiled. If the mast will be stored in-doors, it's a lot easier to leave the wire on it. If your mast rack is outside, try to cover the spar with plastic or cloth wrap. In either case, remove everything that can easily be detached and take it home for cleaning and dust-free storage.

This includes all blocks, lifts and whatever halyards can be extracted. You can usually remove interior halyards by attaching a light line messenger to one end of the halyard (sew the two rope ends together), and then pulling ever so gently on the other. A supply of not-quite-deceased line is handy for a lot of things, by the way—winter halyards, dock lines the yard can lose during haulout and launching, equipment tiedowns. Don't throw short lengths of line away; you'll find a use for them.

Turnbuckles should be disassembled and cleaned with a wire brush once a year. These are secured with cotter rings, instead of pins: With care, rings can be used over and over.

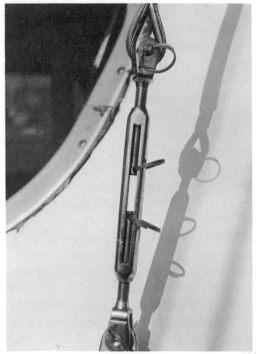

Scrub and wax the mast and boom before storage. Disassemble and wire-brush the turnbuckles, then oil them lightly and store them in a sealed plastic bag at home. Likewise all the blocks and snap shackles—but use a toothbrush to get the grit out of them. Cam cleats and winches will normally require to be cleaned in place, but presumably they will be protected by the boat or mast covering.

Line can be washed in your family washing machine, using warm water and detergent. Be sure first, however, that the lines have no metal fitting at the ends—even a metal thimble can bash around the inside of a washer like a mad thing. Really dirty lines, such as the mainsheet, or lines spliced to wire, such as halyards, will have to be washed by hand and it helps to soak them for a few hours first, to loosen the dirt.

Other maintenance

Ground tackle requires, in general, much the same maintenance as does running rigging. If your anchor rode is normally stowed with a foot or so of its end protruding from the hawsepipe, you should inspect the exposed portion at the end of the season. Line that seems lifeless and dead probably is: cut it off and make a new splice. It is also good practice to swap ends annually, as that will even the wear on the rode.

Don't neglect your mooring rig. If possible, pull the mooring or have a scuba diver inspect it—paying particular attention to the linkage between anchor and chain. You may choose to leave the mooring in place during the winter. But harbors that ice up can destroy a styrofoam buoy in short order. Replace your standard mooring buoy and pickup with a log buoy for winter.

Electronic equipment aboard a boat functions in an inherently hostile environment. It should be removed and taken home to be stored in a warm, dry place—and this should be kept in mind when installing it. Antennas should come off the mast, and you should check with your electronics man about the necessity for replacing the antenna coaxial cable and connectors.

Remove batteries from all battery-powered devices, dust gently inside, and close them up again. I usually turn these slightly used batteries over to the kids and buy all new ones next spring. Any gear requiring overhaul should go to the technicians now, not later. When it comes back, store it in sealed bags containing a dehumidifying agent, such as silica gel.

I have no intention in this limited space of attempting to discuss all the possible problems of inboard and outboard engine maintenance. From extended and sometimes bitter experience, I would make a couple of suggestions, however. First, look at your engine manual. If you don't have one, get one. Read the instructions for winterizing. If they seem completely comprehensible and within your scope, go to it. (This is normally the case with outboard motors.)

If, on the other hand, the instructions seem to have gaps between elements of the same procedure, or if your engine manual is composed of leaflets supplied by the makers of the major parts of the engine, get someone else to winterize it. Whichever path you follow, the instructions, such as they are, should be followed completely.

Maintenance of a boat is no more fun than any other kind of housecleaning, except perhaps for a couple of days early in the spring, when it's too cold for sailing anyway. By careful scheduling and planning, you can at least avoid having to do work twice, and you have a better assurance that your boat will stay in one piece under and over you.

19. Equipment

Various people and organizations publish lists of materiel they feel should be aboard your boat. If you listened to every expert, you'd have no problem because your boat would have sunk from overloading long ago. While it's demonstrably true that certain items are indispensable aboard any boat, a lot of others are needed only once or twice a year, if that. Trouble is, these items are usually emergency equipment, and when you need one of them, you're usually in no position to trot over to the marina store.

I firmly believe in the responsibility of every skipper to decide just how to equip his boat, beyond the legally required minimums. It's your job to know what you need, and nobody can assume it. At the same time, there's nothing wrong with taking advantage of the suggestions of people who've had more experience than you. Just don't be buffaloed by them—examine each recommendation and make up your own mind.

At some point, you'll have to decide enough is enough. You can't carry one of every known safety device, and you wouldn't want to try. There is nothing wrong, I feel, with taking chances as long as you recognize that you're doing it, and have some reasonable idea as to the order of risk involved. Sooner or later on the water you'll have to take a chance, and you might as well have some experience in weighing the odds.

Enough. What follows are three lists, with a few comments of my own, compiled by three august and informed bodies, each concerned with different aspects of venturing out on the water, and each with its own point of vantage.

I: *Minimum Equipment and Accommodations Standards, prepared by the Offshore Rating Council.*
These regulations, prepared for the guidance of clubs and organizations sponsoring offshore races under the IOR, are supplemental to government equipment requirements. Reading the regulations, one should bear in mind two things: first, that they were devised for distance racers, who plan to go out and stay out and even crash around a course in weather that would have a sensible cruising skipper hove-to; and second, that certain items of equipment are included or omitted as part of an overall plan for handicapping racers: Thus some navigational gadgets are left out not because they are useless, but because the racing rules prohibit their employment.

The leaflet, available at modest cost from the North American Yacht Racing Union, was published November 11, 1973.

Offshore Rating Council
Special Regulations Governing Minimum
Equipment and Accommodations Standards

1.0 Purpose and Use

1.1 It is the purpose of these special regulations to establish uniform minimum equipment and accommodations standards for yachts racing under the International Offshore Rule and thereby to aid in promoting uniform offshore racing throughout the world.

1.2 These regulations do not replace, but rather supplement the requirements of governmental authority, the Racing Rules and the International Offshore Rule. The attention of owners is called to restrictions in the rules on the location and movement of equipment.

1.3 The Offshore Rating Council strongly recommends the use of these special regulations by all organizations sponsoring races under the International Offshore Rule. Race Committees may select the category deemed most suitable for the type of race to be sailed. They are urged to depart from the regulations or modify or make exceptions thereto only when the most compelling circumstances so dictate.

2.0 Owner's Responsibility

2.1 The safety of a yacht and her crew is the sole and inescapable responsibility of the owner, who must do his best to insure that the yacht is fully found, thoroughly seaworthy and manned by an experienced crew who are physically fit to face bad weather. He must be satisfied as to the soundness of hull, spars, rigging, sails and all gear. He must insure that all safety equipment is properly maintained and stowed and that the crew know where it is kept and how it is to be used.

2.2 Neither the establishment of these special regulations, their use by the sponsoring organizations, nor the inspection of a yacht under these regulations in any way limits or reduces the complete and unlimited responsibility of the owner.

2.3 It is the sole and exclusive responsibility of each yacht to decide whether or not to start or continue to race.

3.0 Basic Standards

3.1 Hulls of offshore racing yachts shall be self-righting, strongly built, watertight and capable of withstanding solid water and knockdowns. They must be properly rigged and ballasted, be fully seaworthy and must meet the standards set forth herein.

"Self-righting" means that a yacht must have a positive righting arm when the masthead, with main and foresail set, touches the water.

"Properly rigged" means that the shrouds are never to be disconnected.

3.2 All equipment must function properly, be readily accessible and be of a type, size and capacity suitable and adequate for the intended use and the size of the yacht, and shall meet standards acceptable in the country of registry.

4.0 Inspection

4.1 A yacht may be inspected at any time. If she does not comply with these special regulations her entry may be rejected, or she will be liable to disqualification or such other penalty as may be prescribed by national authority or the sponsoring organization.

5.0 Categories of Offshore Events

5.1 The International Offshore Rating Rule is used to rate a wide variety of types and sizes of yachts in many types of races, ranging from long-distance ocean races sailed under adverse conditions to short-course day races sailed in protected waters. To provide for the differences in the standards of safety and accommodation required for such varying circumstances, four categories of races are established, as follows:

5.2 *Category 1 race.* Races of long distance and well offshore, where yachts must be completely self sufficient for extended periods of time, capable of withstanding heavy storms and prepared to meet serious emergencies without the expectation of outside assistance.

5.3 *Category 2 race.* Races of extended duration along or not far removed from shorelines or in large unprotected bays or lakes, where a high degree of self-sufficiency is required of the yachts, but with the reasonable probability that outside assistance could be called upon for aid in the event of serious emergencies.

5.4 *Category 3 race.* Races across open water, most of which is relatively protected or close to shorelines, including races for small yachts.

5.5 *Category 4 race.* Short races, close to shore in relatively warm or protected waters.

In the following lists the [number after an item indicates the category of race for which that item is required.]

6.0 Structural Features

6.1 *Hatches, companionways and ports* must be essentially watertight, that is, capable of being strongly and rigidly secured. Cockpit companionways, if extended below main deck level, must be capable of being blocked off to main deck level. If cockpit opens aft to the sea, the lower edge of the companionway may not be below deck level. 1,2,3,4.

6.2 *Cockpits* must be structurally strong, self-bailing and permanently incorporated as an integral part of the hull. They must be essentially watertight, that is, all openings to the hull below the main deck level must be capable of being strongly and rigidly secured. 1,2,3,4.

6.21 The maximum cockpit volume below lowest coamings shall not exceed 6 percent L times B times FA. The cockpit sole must be at least 2 percent L above LWL. 1.

[Where L is *rated length*, B is *rated beam*, FA is *freeboard aft* and LWL is *waterline length*.]

6.22 The maximum cockpit volume below lowest coamings shall not exceed 9 percent L times B times FA. The cockpit sole must be at least 2 percent L above LWL. 2,3,4.

6.31 *Cockpit drains* adequate to drain cockpit quickly but with a combined area (after allowance for screens, if attached) of not less than the equivalent of two 1'' (2.5 cm) diameter drains. Yachts built after 1-1-72 must have drains with a combined area (after allowance for screens, if attached) of not less than the equivalent of four 3/4'' (2.0 cm) drains. 1,2.

6.32 Cockpit drains adequate to drain cockpit quickly but not less in combined area (after allowance for screens, if attached) than the equivalent of two 1'' (2.5 cm) diameter drains. 3,4.

6.4 *Storm coverings* for all windows more than two square feet in area. 1,2,3.

6.51 *Sea cocks or valves* on all through-hull openings below LWL, except integral deck scuppers, shaft log, speed indicators, depth finders and the like, however a means of closing such openings, when necessary to do so, shall be provided. 1,2,3.

6.52 Soft wood plugs, tapered and of various sizes. 1,2,3,4.

6.6 *Lifelines and pulpits:*

6.61 Fixed bow pulpit (forward of headstay) and stern pulpit (unless lifelines are arranged as to adequately substitute for a stern pulpit). Pulpits and stanchions must be thru-bolted or welded, and the bases thereof must not be further inboard from the edge of the working deck than 5 percent of [maximum beam] or 6 inches (15 cm), whichever is greater. The head of a stanchion must not be angled from the point of its attachment to the hull at more than 10 degrees from vertical throughout the length. Taut double life lines, with upper life line of wire at a height of not less than 2 feet (60 cm) above the working deck, to be permanently supported at intervals of not more than 7 feet (2.15 m). A taut lanyard of synthetic rope may be used to secure lifelines, provided that when in position its

length does not exceed 4 inches (10 cm). Lower lifelines need not extend to the bow pulpit. Lifelines need not be affixed to the bow pulpit if they terminate at, or pass through, adequately braced stanchions 2 feet (60 cm) above the working deck, set inside of and overlapping the bow pulpit, provided that the gap between the upper lifeline and the bow pulpit shall not exceed 6 inches (15 cm). 1,2,3.

6.62 Yachts under 21 feet rating as in 6.61 above, but with a single taut lifeline not less than 18 inches (45 cm) above the working deck, and a bow pulpit and a stern pulpit (unless lifelines are arranged as to adequately substitute for a stern pulpit) to the same height. If the lifeline is at any point more than 22 inches (56 cm) above the rail cap, a second intermediate lifeline must be fitted. If the cockpit opens aft to the sea additional lifelines must be fitted so that no opening is greater in height than 22 inches (56 cm). The bow pulpit may be fitted abaft the forestay with its bases secured at any points on deck, but a point on its upper rail must be within 16 inches (40 cm) of the forestay on which the foremost headsail is hanked. 1,2,3.

6.63 As in 6.61 and 6.62, except that a stern pulpit is not required, provided the required height of lifeline must be carried aft to at least the midpoint of the cockpit. 4.

6.7 *Ballast and Heavy Equipment.* Inside ballast in a yacht shall be securely fastened in position. All other heavy internal fittings such as batteries, stoves, gas bottles, tanks, outboard motors, etc., shall be securely fastened. 1,2,3,4.

7.0 Accommodations

7.11 *Toilet*, permanently installed. 1,2.

7.12 Toilet, permanently installed, or fitted bucket. 3, 4.

7.2 Bunks, permanently installed. 1,2,3,4.

7.31 *Cooking stove*, permanently installed with safe accessible fuel shutoff control. 1,2.

7.32 Cooking stove, capable of being safely operated in a seaway. 3.

7.41 *Galley facilities*, including sink. 1,2.

7.42 Galley facilities. 3,4.

7.51 *Water tanks*, permanently installed and capable of dividing the water supply into at least two separate containers. 1.

7.52 At least one permanently installed water tank, plus at least one additional container capable of holding 2 gallons. 2.

7.53 Water in suitable containers. 3,4.

8.0 General Equipment

8.1 *Fire extinguishers*, readily accessible and of the type and number required by the country of registry, provided there be at least one on yachts fitted with an engine or stove. 1,2,3,4.

8.21 *Bilge pumps*, at least two, manually operated, one of which must be operable with all cockpit seats and all hatches and companionways closed. 1,2.

8.22 One manual bilge pump operable with all cockpit seats, hatches, and companionways closed. 3.

8.23 One manual bilge pump. 4.

8.31 *Anchors*, two with cables except yachts rating under 21 feet, which shall carry at least one such anchor and cable. 1,2,3.

8.32 One anchor and cable. 4.

8.41 *Flashlights*, one of which is suitable for signaling, water resistant, with spare batteries and bulbs. 1,2,3.

8.42 At least one flashlight, water resistant, with spare batteries and bulb. 4.

8.5 *First aid kit* and manual. 1,2,3,4.

8.6 *Foghorn*. 1,2,3,4.

8.7 *Radar reflector*. 1,2,3,4.

8.8 *Set of international code flags* and international code book. 1.

8.9 *Shutoff valves* on all fuel tanks. 1,2,3,4.

9.0 Navigation Equipment

9.1 *Compass*, marine type, properly installed and adjusted. 1,2,3,4.

9.2 *Spare compass*, 1,2,3.

9.3 *Charts, light list and piloting equipment*. 1,2,3.

9.4 *Sextant, tables and accurate time piece*. 1.

9.5 *Radio direction finder*. 1,2.

9.6 *Lead line or echo sounder*. 1,2,3,4.

9.7 *Speedometer or distance measuring instrument*. 1,2,3.

9.8 *Navigation lights*, to be shown as required by the International Regulations for Preventing Collision at Sea, mounted so that they will not be masked by sails or the heeling of the yacht. 1,2,3,4.

10.0 Emergency Equipment

10.1 *Emergency navigation lights* and power source. 1,2.

10.21 *Special storm sail(s)* capable of taking the yacht to windward in heavy weather. 1,2.

10.22 Heavy weather jib and reefing equipment for mainsail. 3,4.

10.3 *Emergency steering equipment*. 1,2,3.

10.4 *Tools and spare parts*, including a hacksaw. 1,2,3,4.

10.5 *Yacht's name* on miscellaneous buoyant equipment, such as life jackets, oars, cushions, etc. Portable sail number. 1,2,3.

10.61 *Marine radio transmitter and receiver*, with minimum transmitter power of 25 watts. If the regular antenna depends upon the mast, an emergency antenna must be provided. 1.

10.62 *Radio receiver* capable of receiving weather bulletins. 2,3,4.

11.0 Safety Equipment

11.1 *Life jackets*, one for each crew member. 1,2,3,4.

11.2 *Whistles* attached to the life jackets. 1,2,3.

11.3 *Safety belt* (harness type) one for each crew member. 1,2,3.

11.41 *Life raft(s)* capable of carrying the entire crew and meeting ,the following requirements: 1,2,3.

Must be carried on deck (not under a dinghy) or in a special stowage opening immediately to the deck containing life raft(s) only:

Must be designed and used solely for saving life at sea;

Must have at least two separate buoyancy compartments, each of which must be automatically inflatable; each raft must be capable of carrying its rated capacity with one compartment deflated;

Must have a canopy to cover the occupants;

Must have been inspected, tested and approved within two years by the manufacturer or other competent authority; and

Must have the following equipment appropriately secured to each raft.

Although not listed in any organization's safety equipment recommendations, the through-bolted steps on the rudder of this Dreadnought Tahiti ketch could easily save the life of a man overboard. And you don't need a separate ladder.

1 Sea anchor or drogue
1 Bellows, pump or other means for maintaining inflation of air chambers
1 Signaling light
3 Hand flares
1 Baler
1 Repair kit
2 Paddles
1 Knife

11.42 Provision for emergency water and rations to accompany raft. 1.

11.51 *Life ring(s)*, at least one horseshoe type life ring equipped with a waterproof light and drogue within reach of the helmsman and ready for instant use. 4.

11.52 At least one horseshoe type life ring equipped with a self-igniting high-intensity water light and a drogue within reach of the helmsman and ready for instant use. 1,2,3.

11.53 At least one more horseshoe type life ring equipped with a whistle, dye marker, drogue, a self-igniting high intensity water light, and a pole and flag. The pole is to be attached to the ring with

25 feet (8 m) of floating line and is to be of a length and so ballasted that the flag will fly at least 8 feet (2.45 m) off the water. 1,2.

11.61 *Distress signals* to be stowed in a waterproof container and meeting the following requirements for each category, as indicated: 1,2,3,4.

11.62 Twelve red parachute flares. 1.

11.63 Four red parachute flares. 2,3.

11.64 Four red hand flares. 1,2,3,4.

11.65 Four white hand flares. 1,2,3,4.

11.7 *Heaving line* (50 foot (16 m) minimum length, floating type line) readily accessible to cockpit. 1,2,3,4.

II: Recommendations for Safety Equipment for Sea-going Craft below 45 ft. L.O.A., prepared by the Royal Yachting Association.

The RYA is a bit difficult to explain to American readers, as we have no direct comparison. It functions as a standards-setting body, lobbying organization, educational group and racing promoter, and also derives some of its stature from its Royal sanction, a form of endorsement wholly baffling to most U.S. citizens. The booklet from which these recommendations derive was published in September 1972. Like the regulations of the ORC, these lists are *in addition to* national and international equipment requirements. They are aimed at mariners operating in the rough waters around the United Kingdom, but are not intended to replace racing equipment regulations.

I have edited the list slightly, omitting gear which applies only to powerboats, and the names of British authorities approving equipment.

Personal Safety Equipment

Safety Harnesses—1 for each person on sailing yachts.

Wear a safety harness on deck in bad weather or at night. Make sure it is properly adjusted.

Experience has shown, however, that a harness may be dangerous if you go overboard at speeds of 8 knots or more.

Life jackets—1 for each person.

Keep them in a safe place where you can get at them easily. Always wear one when there is a risk of being pitched overboard.

Rescue Equipment for Man Overboard

Lifebuoys—2 at least.

One lifebuoy should be kept within easy reach of the helmsman. For sailing at night, it should be fitted with a self-igniting light.

Buoyant line within helmsman's reach.

30 meters (100 feet) (minimum breaking strain of 115 kilos (250 lbs.)).

Other Flotation Equipment for Vessels Going More Than 3 Miles Out, Summer and Winter

Inflatable Life Raft—to carry everyone on board.

To be carried on deck or in a locker opening directly to the deck. It should be serviced annually.

Or

Rigid Dinghy—with permanent, not inflatable, buoyancy, and with oars and rowlocks secured.

To be carried on deck. It may be a collapsible type.

Or

Inflatable Dinghy—built with two compartments, one at least always kept fully inflated, or built with one compartment, always kept fully inflated, and having oars and rowlocks secured.

To be carried on deck. If the vessel has enough permanent buoyancy to float when swamped with 115 kilos (250 lbs.) added weight, a dinghy with two compartments may be stowed.

In sheltered waters, a dinghy may be towed. Check that the tow is secure.

For Vessels Going Not More Than 3 Miles Out, In Winter (1 November to 31 March)

Inflatable Life Raft or alternatives, as above.

In sheltered waters the summer scale equipment, listed below, may usually be adequate.

146

For Vessels Going Not More Than 3 Miles Out, In Summer (1 April to 31 October)

30 in. Lifebuoys or Buoyant Seats—1 for every two people on board.

Lifebuoys carried for "man overboard" situations may be included. Those smaller than 30 in. diameter should be regarded as support for one person only.

General Equipment

Two Anchors—Each with warp or chain of appropriate size and length. Where warp is used at least 5.5 meters (3 fathoms) of chain should be used between anchor and warp.

Bilge Pump

Efficient Compass, and spare

Charts covering intended area of operation

Distress Flares, 6 with 2 of the rocket parachute type

Daylight Distress (Smoke) Signals

Two Ropes, of adequate length

First Aid Box with Anti-Seasickness Tablets

Radio Receiver, for weather forecasts

Water-Resistant Torch

Radar Reflector, of adequate performance

As large as can be carried conveniently. Preferably mounted at least 3 meters (10 feet) above sea level.

Lifeline

Also useful in bad weather for inboard lifelines.

Engine Tool Kit

Name, Number or generally recognized *Sail Number*

Should be painted prominently on the vessel or on dodgers in letters or figures at least 22 centimeters (9 inches) high.

Fire Fighting Equipment

For vessels over 9 meters (30 feet) in length, and those with powerful engines, carrying quantities of fuel.

Fire Extinguishers

2, each of not less than 1.4 kilos (3 lbs.) capacity, dry powder, or equivalent and 1 or more additional extinguishers of not less than 2.3 kilos (5 lbs.) capacity, dry powder, or equivalent.

For vessels of up to 9 meters (30 feet) in length, with cooking facilities and engines.

2, each of not less than 1.4 kilos (3 lbs.) capacity, dry powder, or equivalent.

For vessels up to 9 meters (30 feet) in length, with cooking facilities only or with engine only.

1, of not less than 1.4 kilos (3 lbs.) capacity, dry powder, or equivalent.

Carbon dioxide (CO_2) or foam extinguishers of equal extinguishing capacity are alternatives to dry powder appliances.

Additionally, for all craft:

Buckets, with lanyard

2, on each vessel.

Bag of Sand

Useful in containing and extinguishing burning spillage of fuel or lubricant.

III. U.S. Coast Guard Auxiliary Courtesy Motorboat Examination and Federal Equipment Check.

As most experienced boat owners are aware, the civilian volunteers who comprise the U.S. Coast Guard Auxiliary provide as a free service to the boat owner the Courtesy Motorboat Examination. Upon the owner's request, an Auxiliary Examiner will check out the craft according to the following list of legal requirements and additional Auxiliary standards. Boats meeting both sets of standards are awarded an annually dated decal which will normally exempt them from examination under way by the Coast Guard or other law enforcement body; if the boat fails to pass, the owner is privately advised of the deficiency, but no report is made to the Coast Guard or the marine police.

Federal Requirements

1. Identification and Numbering—Papers are in order. Numbers block type, proper size, properly spaced, distinctly visible. Name and Hailing Port displayed and Official Number

The Hull Identification Number (HIN) is stamped into this fiberglass transom. The combination of letters and numbers indicates the builder, boat serial number, date of construction.

marked on main beam (documented yacht only).

2. Hull Identification Number—Proper location, proper display (boats for which construction began after 10/31/72).

3. Display of Capacity Information—Proper location, proper display (if required) (boats for which construc tion began after 10/31/72).

4. Certification of Compliance—Proper location, proper display (if required) (boats for which construction began after 10/31/72).

5. Bell—Boats 26 feet and over in length.

Combined Federal and (Auxiliary) Requirements

6. Personal Flotation Devices—Approved type—Required number, satisfactory condition, readily accessible. (One approved personal flotation device for each person on board but not less than one for each bunk or less than two.)

7. Ventilation—Adequate; each engine and fuel tank compartment. Boats built after 4/25/40. (Conforms with Auxiliary standards regardless of date of construction.)

8. Backfire Flame Control—Properly attached to each carburetor of each gasoline engine, except outboard engines, installed after 4/25/40. (Satisfactory installation required; except outboard engines, regardless of date of construction.)

9. Fire Extinguishers—Approved type. Ade-

147

quate in size & number.* Satisfactory condition; readily accessible. Except outboards of open construction under 26 feet in length. (One portable unit in boats up to 26 feet in length regardless of construction or fixed fire extinguishing system.)

10. Whistle or Other Sound Producing Device—Adequate; meets Federal requirement for class of boat on which installed. All boats of 16 foot length or longer. (Required for all boats.)

11. Navigational lights—Display required underway between sunset and sunrise, white green, red. White when anchored. (Running and anchor lights installed and operating satisfactorily.)

Additional Auxiliary Requirements

12. Portable Fuel Tanks and Containers—Condition satisfactory, free of leaks, properly stowed.

13. Permanently Installed Fuel Tanks—Condition and installation satisfactory. Fill pipe tight to deck plate, located outside coaming or within self-bailing cockpit. Fuel tank vents leading outboard.

14. Carburetor Drip Collector—Installed satisfactorily to prevent spill into bilge.

15. Electrical Installation—Wiring in good condition, circuits fused, no knife switches in bilge, batteries properly installed.

16. Distress Flare—Preferably hand-held red flares, fuse type or burning torch. Check state law for required permit on other types such as Very pistols, signal guns, flare guns, etc.

17. Galley stove—Marine type, properly installed.

18. Paddle or Oar—Required for boats under 16 feet only.

19. Manual Pump or Bailer—Required for boats under 16 feet only.

20. Anchor and Anchor Line—Suitable size and length for vessel and operating area.

21. General Condition—Vessel in good overall condition, bilges clean, free from fire hazards. Bilge pumps operable.

*For most boatmen, who use the dry chemical type, this means one extinguisher containing at least 2-1/2 pounds of chemical for boats under 26 feet; two extinguishers for boats 26 up to 40 feet; three for boats over 40 feet.

The Auxiliary also recommends the following additional equipment or installations, although they are not required in order to receive the CME decal:

Through hull fittings should have shut-off valves or wooden plugs accessible for use.

Fuel lines must lead from the top of the tank and be equipped with shut off valves at the tank and engine.

Auxiliary generators should have separate, permanently installed fuel tanks.

Switches should not be located in bilges.

Distress signaling equipment should be carried on every boat.

A manual bilge pump should be carried on every boat, irrespective of any mechanical pumping devices.

Handrails should be secured with through bolts.

Spare canisters should be carried for horns or whistles which operate from compressed gas.

Spare batteries and spare bulbs should be carried for battery operated lights.

A fully equipped first aid kit should be carried in every boat.

Have tools and spare parts on board in usable condition.

On the same form, the Auxiliary supplies a checklist of desirable equipment to have aboard "depending on size, location and use of boat." Although intended for all sizes of boat, it makes a good, basic checklist, so I include it intact:

Anchors (1 light, 1 heavy)
Anchor Chain or Line (long)
Barometer
Bilge Pumps
Binoculars
Boat Hook
Chamois
Coast Pilot
Compass
Course Protractor or Parallel Rules
Deck Swab
Deviation Table
Direction Finder, Radio

Distress Signals
  Flashlight
  Signaling Mirror
  Smoke Signals
  Water Dye Marker
Dividers
Emergency Rations and Water
Fenders
First Aid Kit and Manual
Heaving Line
Insect Repellent
Lantern
Leadline (for soundings)
Local Charts
Light List
Megaphone

Mooring Lines
Motor Crank Handle
Motor Oil and Grease (extra)
Nails, Screws, Bolts, Pins, Washers, Wire, Tape
Patent Log
Pelorus
Radio Telephone
Ring Buoys
R.P.M. Table
Searchlight
Spare Batteries
Spare Propeller
Sunglasses
Sunburn Lotion
Sunburn Preventive
Spare Parts
  Coil
  Condenser
  Distributor Head
  Distributor Points
  Distributor Rotor
  Fuel Pump Repair Kit
  Fuses
  Light Bulbs
  Spark Plugs
Tools
Water Pump

The Ditty Bag

It's very hard to separate completely the components of the ship's toolbox, the spare parts box and the sailor's ditty bag. What follows is my own list, developed over several boats, of items I have found either useful or indispensable. Some are spares, some are tools which could also be used in engine repair. I keep most of them in a large, vinyl drawstring bag with half a dozen outside pockets, and the items pertaining strictly to sail and rope work in a separate, smaller bag.

Crescent wrench
Slip joint pliers
Vise grip pliers
Hacksaw with extra blades
Small hammer
Screwdriver socket with assorted standard and
  Phillips blades
Nonmagnetic screwdriver
18″ stainless steel shroud wire, with 4 bulldog
  clips (for emergency stay and shroud repair)
8-foot steel tape
Rat-tail file
Hand drill with assorted bits
Electrical tape
Waterproof sail tape
Waterproof heavy tape
Galvanized wire (for wiring shackle pins)
Extra wool for telltales
Assorted screws, bolts, machine screws, washers
  in 35 mm. film cases
Penetrating oil
Lubricating oil
Waterproof grease
Assorted sail needles
Waxed whipping thread
Dacron sail thread
Cotton line, for stopping spinnaker
Tarred line
Fid (the Swedish design cutaway tube) [for
  splicing]
Beeswax
Sailmaker's palm
Assorted thimbles, plastic and galvanized
Assorted shackles, bronze, galvanized (for
  ground tackle), stainless (for rigging), includ-
  ing spare main halyard shackle
Assorted cotter rings and pins, bronze and
  stainless

Extra blocks—one single, one fiddle, one lightweight for flag halyards, etc.

Swiss Army-type pocketknife (the little scissors are the most consistently useful attachment)

Knife sharpening stone

Sheepsfoot sheath knife with marlinspike

It's a lot of stuff, to be sure, but I've used all of it from time to time, and have been happy I had it.

Running Rigging Inventory

The following list of running rigging and spares, for the author's 23-foot catamaran sloop, is obviously not going to be transferrable to all other craft—or even to all boats of the same general size and rig. It is included here as a tolerably complete selection of what the boat owner can expect to have to buy, either in the standard boat or as optional extras.

Mainsail

Halyard—60 ft. prestretched Dacron 3/8" Diam. w/captive pin SS shackle.

Downhaul—20 ft. Dacron 5/16" Diam. w/4-part, self-jamming block system.

Boom vang—30 ft. 3/8" Dacron w/4-part block system and integral cam cleat; secured to captive pin shackle for deck fittings, Nicro plate-and-strap vang attachment.

Sheet—40 ft. prestretched Dacron braid 3/8" Diam. w/4-part block system and integral cam cleat; running on 9-foot track adjustable w/built-in block system.

Jibs

Halyard—60 ft. prestretched Dacron 3/8" Diam. w/SS swivel snap shackle.

Tack—SS swivel snap shackle w/one 12" and one 18" SS wire extenders to raise jib foot.

Heavy Sheet—2 40-foot lengths of laid Dacron 3/8" Diam.

Ultralight Sheet—2 40-foot lengths of 1/8" Dacron braid.

Semicircular rings welded to the pulpit are an excellent place to dead-end halyard snap shackles.

Blocks—4 nylon shell blocks (two foot, two turning) on sliding cars.

Spinnaker

Halyard—60 ft. 3/8" laid Dacron w/SS swivel snap shackle, running through masthead swivel block.

Sheets—2 40-foot lengths of 5/16" Dacron w/2 SS snap hooks, running through two SS quarter blocks w/nylon sheaves.

Spinnaker Pole Lift—25 ft. 5/16" Dacron w/bronze snap running through SS swivel block.

Pole Downhaul—25 ft. 5/16" Dacron w/captive pin shackle running through SS swivel block.

Miscellaneous

Flag Halyards—1 60 ft., 1 30-ft. of 1/8" Dacron.

Topping Lift—60-ft. Dacron 5/16" Diam. w/SS shackle.

Spare Sheet—40 ft. prestretched Dacron braid 3/8" Diam.

Spare Blocks—1 each SS fiddle block, double block, single block, for 3/8" line.

Spare Halyard Shackle—SS captive pin.

The amount of line required to control a spinnaker is probably double what's needed for any other sail.

Bibliography

Beiser, Arthur, *The Proper Yacht*, New York.

Blanchard, Fessenden S. *The Sailboat Classes of North America*. Garden City, N.Y.: Doubleday & Co., 1968 (revised).

Bowker, R.M. and Budd, S.A. *Make Your Own Sails*. New York: St. Martin's Press, 1959.

Brown, Alan. *Invitation to Sailboat Racing*. New York: Simon & Schuster, 1972.

Choy, Rudy. *Catamarans Offshore*. New York: Macmillan, 1970.

Colvin, Thomas, E. *Coastwise and Offshore Cruising Wrinkles*. New York: Seven Seas Press, 1972.

Cotter, Edward F. *Multihull Sailboats*. New York: Crown Publishers, 1966.

Duffett, John. *Modern Marine Maintenance*. New York: Motor Boating & Sailing Books, 1973.

Elvstrom, Paul. *Expert Dinghy and Keelboat Racing*. Chicago: Quadrangle Books, 1967.

Falk, Stephen. *The Fundamentals of Sailboat Racing*. New York: St. Martin's Press, 1973.

Falk, Stephen. *Sailing Racing Rules the Easy Way*. New York: St. Martin's Press, 1972.

Giannoni, Frances and Giannoni, John. *Useful Knots and Line Handling*. New York: Golden Press, 1968.

Gibbs, Tony. *Pilot's Work Book*. New York: Seven Seas Press, 1972.

Gibbs, Tony. *Practical Sailing*. New York: Motor Boating & Sailing Books, 1971.

Gray, Alan. *Marconi Rigging and Sailmaking*. New York: Rudder Publishing Co., 1934.

Henderson, Richard. *The Cruiser's Compendium*. Chicago: Henry Regnery Co., 1973.

Henderson, Richard. *The Racing-Cruiser*. Chicago: Reilly & Lee, 1970.

Henderson, Richard, *Sea Sense*. Camden, Maine: International Marine Publishing Co., 1972.

Hiscock, Eric C., *Voyaging Under Sail*. New York: Oxford University Press, 1959.

Howard-Williams, Jeremy. *Sails*. Tuckahoe, N.Y.: John de Graff, Inc., 1971.

Illingworth, John. *Offshore*. London: Adlard Coles Ltd., 1953.

Johnson, Peter, *Ocean Racing & Offshore Yachts*. New York: Dodd, Mead Co., 1970.

Johnson, Peter. *Yachtsman's Guide to the Rating Rule*. Chicago: Quadrangle Books, 1972.

Kals, W.S. *Practical Boating*. Garden City, N.Y.: Doubleday & Co., 1969.

Leather, John. *Gaff Rig*. London: Adlard Coles, Ltd., 1970.

McCollam, Jim. *The Yachtsman's Weather Manual*. New York: Dodd, Mead Co., 1973.

Marchaj, C.A. *Sailing Theory and Practice*. New York: Dodd, Mead Co., 1964.

Oakeley, John D.A. *Winning: The Boat, the Crew and the Race*. Chicago: Quadrangle Books, 1970.

Phillips-Birt, Douglas. *A History of Seamanship*. Garden City, N.Y.: Doubleday & Co., 1971.

Phillips-Birt, Douglas. *Sailing Yacht Design*. London: Adlard Coles Ltd., 1966.

Robinson, Bill (ed.). *The Science of Sailing*. New York: Charles Scribner's Sons, 1961.

Ross, Wallace. *Sail Power*. New York: Alfred A. Knopf, 1974.

Smith, Hervey Garrett. *The Arts of the Sailor*. New York: Funk & Wagnalls, 1968.

Watts, Alan. *Wind and Sailing Boats*. Chicago: Quadrangle Books, 1970.

White, Reg, and Fisher, Bob. *Catamaran Racing*. Tuckahoe, N.Y.: John de Graff, Inc., 1968.

Zadig, Ernest A. *The Boatman's Guide to Modern Marine Materials*. New York: Motor Boating & Sailing Books , 1974.